THE BIG BUTT BLESSING

How Hating My Body Led to Loving My Life

Cover art courtesy of Sunny Rosanbalm.

First published by Dog Ear Publishing
4010 W. 86th Street, Ste H
Indianapolis, IN 46268
www.dogearpublishing.net

ISBN: 978-160844-238-6

This book is printed on acid-free paper.

Printed in the United States of America

Contents

For Carli: My sweet beauty from ashes

Introduction

As I sit here contemplating the contents of this book, my heart is filled with thanksgiving beyond words. You see, for much of my life, I lived with an almost constant cloud of doom hanging over my head. There was an emotional heaviness and sense of despair deeply ingrained into the core of my identity. No matter what my friends and family would say, I believed there was nothing special about my life, and I had little hope that my future would hold anything beyond ordinary. To make things worse, I hated the way I looked. I could not stand looking at myself in the mirror for any length of time, and the sense of disgust I felt for my own flesh contaminated every area of my life. But all of that has changed.

At a time when I had only one ounce of desire to live, truth got a hold of me and shook me to the core. God's heavenly flashlight brought light one area at a time to parts of my heart that desperately needed hope and healing. I began to see that much of my outlook on life was based on lies—lies I had been told by the enemy of my soul and lies I had been telling myself. At first I felt like a fool for being so easily influenced by lies, but my embarrassment soon lead to righteous anger and a desire to absorb truth into every fiber of my being—and a desire to kick my enemy in the tail!

Today, nothing much has changed about my outward appearance, but my insides have been radically transformed. I love who God made me to be, and I'm excited about my future. It's ironic that the peace and joy I now feel might not have come if I had not so desperately hated my body. Every tear I cried while looking into the mirror brought me one step closer to the desperation that would finally bring me to total surrender. This is why I can say that my big butt is a blessing.

This book is written for two reasons: first, it is a small offering of thanks to my Heavenly Daddy, whose amazing love brings me to my knees; second, it is a testimony of amazing freedom that I pray might bring encouragement and hope to someone else. It has been and will continue to be a process, but what I share in this book is my heart's cry. I once was lost in self-hatred and depression, but now I am found in the unconditional love and adoration of my Heavenly Father, and I love who He has chosen to make me. I hope you will join me in this place!

Note: All scripture references in this book are taken from the New King James Version.

PART ONE

BELIEVING A LIE

CHAPTER ONE

THE ENEMY IN THE MIRROR

There are enemies all around us
Seeking to destroy.
They come to tear our hearts apart
And take away our joy.
Some are just plain bothersome,
Some invoke great fear.
But none are near as devastating
As the enemy in the mirror.

I don't recall even one season of my life when looking in the mirror was a positive experience. It seems that even at a young age, my reflection was not a friend. I can remember squeezing my thighs to see what they would look like if I could just lose one inch off both sides. Or sucking in my stomach and wishing I looked like that when I was relaxed. Or I would go to the opposite extreme; I would jump up and down just to watch my fat jiggle and then ridicule myself. Either way, I was pretty disgusted with what I saw. I didn't realize it at first, but a toxic relationship was developing between me and the person in the mirror. We were becoming enemies.

My preoccupation with my physical appearance began in grade school. I can remember my first grade classmates, especially the boys, making fun of my very long, thick hair and my rotten front teeth. By second grade, it was my weight they were making fun of. It's funny, but when I look back at pictures of myself, I don't appear fat at all. I was a little bigger than some of the other girls my age, but I was far from being a fat child. Reality is invisible to children, however. In my world, if they said I was fat, it must be true.

To make matters worse, my childhood best friend was rail thin. I can remember sitting next to her on the benches in the cafeteria at lunchtime and noticing how much wider the spread of my thigh was than hers. I would try to adjust the way I was sitting to make my leg appear as small as it could, but it would never get thin enough. At that age I had no understanding of bone size and metabolic type; all I understood was that the boys seemed to think my friend was beautiful because she was skinny, and that left me out of the running. When I left grade school to go on to seventh grade, one lesson I had learned and retained was that being beautiful meant being thin.

Middle school was the fertilizer for the seeds of my emergent self-loathing. What had been somewhat hurtful before became flat-out devastating to me. Suddenly, not only did the size of my butt matter, but the jeans I wore to cover it had to be Ralph Lauren or Calvin Klein. Because my family wasn't rolling in cash, my jeans were usually from Target or J.C. Penney. The looks of disdain and the rejection I received in that learning institution penetrated deep into my self-image.

I can remember being desperately concerned with what the "in crowd" thought of me. My mom (bless her heart) would buy name brand clothes from rich people's garage sales, take off the labels, and then sew them onto brand new shirts from J.C. Penney just to keep me from despair. From the moment I would sit down in class I was hyper-aware of what I looked like to my peers. "Does the way I'm sitting make me look fat?" "Is the guy behind me looking at my rear?" Sometimes I'm amazed that I passed any of my classes, being so concerned with how I appeared to others.

The Loophole

In high school I learned a new lesson: You can bypass the "thin equals beauty" law if you are willing to let a boy have his way with you. Once again, my new best friend was much thinner than I was, and she was always getting attention from the boys. Being as desperately lost in the abyss of self-loathing as I was, this newfound loophole seemed like my only way to keep up with her. I hated the girl I saw in the mirror, and by then, she was always quick to remind me that no boy would ever find me attractive. So I grabbed all the attention I could get by whatever means necessary. Of course, this was an evil deception, because with each passing year, my shame and humiliation grew stronger, and, of course, so did my hatred for my reflection.

There were a few times in my early 20s that I lost some weight and thought I was close to being beautiful. My seasons of being slimmer would not last long, however, and even though I knew the loophole I had found in high school was a fluke, I hadn't found any other way to gain the attention of men. I resigned myself to remain in the insanity of promiscuity, hoping that I would find someone to love me. The girl in the mirror wouldn't even look at me sometimes.

By God's good grace, I hit rock bottom by the time I was 21 years old. I had been doing such a lousy job ruling my life that it became very apparent I needed to surrender the throne. I vividly remember the night before Jesus took over, which is a miracle, because I was extremely intoxicated. During my last reigning night, I got in a fight with my best friend (who was yet another girl much thinner than I) because I thought she was trying to steal my boyfriend. The bouncers at the party I was attending had to throw me out, and my boyfriend was most definitely done with me. My ruling days ended with a bang.

Over the course of the next 14 or so years, I began to accept the forgiveness that God had for me because of Jesus dying on the cross. I began to see that my life had value and that there was a plan for me. I met new friends and totally changed my lifestyle. Things were definitely getting better. I was excited to be alive, and many of the lies I had believed in my past were being dispelled. All but one. I still couldn't believe that I was beautiful unless I was thin, and even though we were on speaking terms again, the girl in the mirror didn't think so, either.

Less than God's Best

When Jesus took the throne in my life, I was on fire. I couldn't wait to get off work to rush home to read the Bible. For the first time, the words were making some sense to me. Eventually, I started attending a church that I loved, and I learned more and more of the truth of God's Word. One special lesson I remember the Father gently teaching me was the reason why He intended for people to save sex for marriage. This lesson impacted me so deeply because it was an issue I had grappled with for so many years. I remembered knowing somewhere deep within my little-girl heart that sex should be saved for marriage, but that innate knowledge had been slowly squelched by the lies I had chosen to believe. My ignorance of God's heart eventually led me to ignore the whole "wait until marriage" concept. I had to ignore it to be able to live with myself. But He lovingly showed me that His reason for designing sex for marriage was to protect my heart. "I never intended for you to carry the shame and emotional baggage you carry," He lovingly impressed on my heart. "It's not that I want to rob you of fun." I was overwhelmed with grief over what I had done in my past, but Father God was good enough to wash me with His love and forgiveness.

Even though my understanding was limited, I was beginning to experience God's love and healing power. My life was changing in many ways, including where I lived. I moved across the country from California to Tennessee to be closer to my family, and as soon as I arrived, I started looking for a new church. It took several tries before I found one that seemed comfortable for me, but I quickly settled in.

Contrary to the way things had been at my California church, outward appearance seemed to be important at this one. The pastor's wife and daughter were always wearing the best clothes—a different outfit every Sunday, it seemed. In addition to that, they were both nice and thin. Despite the new friendships I was making and the spiritual growth that was occurring in my life, I still felt inadequate because of my weight. Deep inside, I related much of my worth to the size of my pants, and my low self-esteem led me to make some painfully wrong decisions.

At age 24, I met the man who would soon become my first husband. He was a member at my church; in fact, he was an usher there. I took this to mean he was a great catch. I remember thinking he was very cute and wanting to get to know him. Eventually, I learned that he suffered with drug and alcohol problems, but I felt much compassion and wanted to tell him that God could fix that.

I got to know him more, and soon we were officially dating. I was overjoyed and amazed that he liked me, because, after all, I wasn't the thinnest girl in the place. The false sense of security I had because of his interest in me soon became overshadowed by my growing awareness of his problems. They were pretty serious, but I didn't let that scare me off. I just knew I was meant to help save him. The girl in the mirror was pretty insistent that I stay with him, too. "This might be the last time you'll find someone who actually thinks you're pretty," she would say.

Despite the warnings of my family and closest friends, I accepted an offer of engagement and began planning for a wedding. At some point during our engagement, my fiancé was put into a 30-day alcohol and drug treatment program. The warnings from my family grew more vehement, but the girl in the mirror kept insisting that this was the best I could do, so I turned my back on logical thinking and plunged myself into standing by my man. I desperately hoped he would change and that I would show the world I was right about him. My prideful but low self-esteem was a masterful deceiver.

From the moment I said "I do," something deep inside me knew I had made a terrible mistake. There was nothing I could do about it by then, so I put my heart and soul into making my marriage work. My new husband did stay sober for a short season, but within a few months, he had relapsed. I was devastated but kept believing in miracles.

Two months after we were married, I found out I was pregnant. Reading "positive" on that home pregnancy test was a bittersweet moment. I was thrilled to have a baby on the way, but I was painfully miserable in my marriage. My heart was breaking more and more with every relapse my husband experienced, and my pain and shame caused me to pull even further away from my family and friends. I was scared of what the future would hold for me and my baby. All I wanted was a godly marriage and for my husband to be healed, but it didn't happen that way for me.

Within three years, my marriage was over. Despite several attempts at sobriety, my husband just could not stay healthy. Our relationship had deteriorated so much that there was no trust left, and I could not stand to let my daughter experience the dysfunction any longer. Because I knew separating for a season was okay with God, I chose to move in with my parents for a while to see what would happen. What happened was a divorce. After that, I could barely face the girl in the mirror anymore. Not only was I too fat, but I was a failure and an idiot. I wondered how God could possibly use me in His kingdom ever again.

Date Nights with Jesus

Near the time my divorce was made final, I moved to the family student housing complex at a state college in Tennessee. It was a quaint little 450-square-foot apartment just big enough for my 3-year-old daughter and me to start our new life together. I was attending classes in pursuit of my teaching degree and working three part-time jobs. The Lord blessed me with a day care right on campus for my daughter to attend two days a week while I went to classes. The rest of the week, she was with me, lending me her sweet, innocent companionship and devotion.

My days were spent busily taking care of school work and my daughter, but my nights were spent mostly in tears. I was wreaked with the realization that all my hopes and dreams had died. I was now without a husband, and even though I wasn't really thinking about having another chance, I was pretty sure that no one would ever want a chubby single mom. I began trying to lose some weight because I was surrounded every day by skinny college girls several years my junior. Everywhere I looked, I was reminded of how far I fell below the mark.

Despite my weight struggles, my personality started to come back after a while. I found myself enjoying life a little and getting back into spending time with old friends and family. I put my heart and soul into being the best mom I could be for my daughter, spending much time holding her and thanking God for her life. But still, when nighttime came, the loneliness and shame would creep back in, nearly swallowing me up like a vulture with fresh road kill. Sometimes my mind would wander way out into the future, and I would become filled with anxiety and fear that nothing would ever change, that although things were better for me, this was as good as it would ever be. I was desperate for answers and a glimpse of hope. It was during that season that Jesus showed up one night to ask me out on a date.

I know it may seem weird to say that I was asked out by the Lord, but I really was. Of course He didn't appear physically at my door, but He did appear to my heart and soul in a tangible way. I could not deny that He wanted my full attention. I also knew I must invite Him in. We never actually left my apartment for our dates; we just sat on the couch and talked. I realize it may seem a bit crazy, but there were times when I could honestly feel His arm around my shoulders and the adoration flowing from His heart. I poured out my soul to Him, admitting all my fears and confessing my insecurities. All I received in return was His professed love for me time and time again. It was tangible—warm. Jesus had become my boyfriend. I could sense that He actually wanted to pursue me and date me. This was a totally new idea, but it felt wonderful, and I wanted all I could get. Nothing was better.

For the next several months, it seemed most nights were date nights with the Lord. I began to understand that He was the one and only true lover of my soul. He was my lover! Even though it sometimes felt odd to think of Jesus that way, I knew it was a pure and holy love, and it was a safe place for me. I knew Jesus thought I was radiant, and He didn't care how much I weighed.

The problem was, no matter how Jesus saw me, other men didn't seem to see me through His eyes. The girl in the mirror didn't, either. We still had a problem looking at each other.

God of Second Chances

My season of being a single mom did not last as long as I had been certain it would, which is funny, because I was truly beginning to enjoy my new life, having Jesus as a boyfriend. Though there were times when I craved physical touch and wished that I could really feel Jesus touching me, most of the time, I felt genuinely at peace.

Despite all the love Jesus was lavishing on me, there were times when the fear and insecurity about my future would take center stage in my mind again. It was easy for me to fall into a trap of self-pity when I allowed myself to go there.

I remember one such time. I was having a major self-pity and fear party. I was truly afraid that this life would be nothing more than mediocre for me and that any really great things would happen only in heaven. I envisioned myself as a lonely 80-year-old woman dutifully waiting for the Rapture. I would make the best of this life, of course, but nothing really fun would happen for me.

The Holy Spirit didn't let me stay in that emotionally lost place for long. As I was reading the Bible one morning, I found myself reading in the book of Psalms. I read a scripture and heard an almost audible voice tell me it was for me. The words, given life by the love of God, changed my life.

As I read those words of King David, I imagined that he must have been having a moment somewhat like mine, one filled with despair and fear of the future. It is obvious from what he writes that he has received some direct revelation from God and has been comforted. Because of the comfort he received, this is what he says: *"I would have lost heart, unless I had believed that I would see the goodness of the Lord in the land of the living" (Psalm 27:13).*

King David knew that the Lord's goodness wasn't just stored up in heaven to be experienced only after death; he knew that God's goodness was to be seen during his life. Through David's words, the Lord was telling me that it was ridiculous for me to think He would withhold good things from me until I died. He was telling me He did have good things for me to be had while I was alive. It didn't take Him long to prove it.

Even though it may be an overused comparison, what happened next in my life was like a true Cinderella story. I met a man named Bill at my new church one day. Bill had moved to Tennessee from Oregon. I heard through the grapevine that he was a 27-year-old virgin (see what girls talk about at church), and even though I'm embarrassed to say it, my best friend and I had a good laugh about that. We weren't laughing because we thought it was silly; in fact, we felt the exact opposite. We were impressed. We were laughing because the thought of anyone that righteous desiring either one of us for a wife seemed an absurdity.

I remember thinking Bill was a cute guy, but I didn't really think much more about him at first. After all, what would a cute, godly man want with a used up, chubby single mom? I didn't even entertain the idea of getting to know him because it was so obviously out of the question. I wasn't really sure if a second marriage was what God wanted for me, anyway, and I was intent on doing things God's way to the best of my ability.

It didn't take long before circumstances put us together in conversation. We talked for hours, discovering the many things we had in common. Our goals, personalities, and dreams were very similar, and there was never a shortage of things to talk about. Eventually, we began officially dating. It was February when we had our first real date, and by May, we were engaged. I couldn't believe what was happening to me. It was very hard to accept.

I was painfully aware that this man who had managed to save himself for marriage was getting the short end of the stick. How could I possibly be the prize he had been keeping himself for? Didn't a man like that deserve a woman with a firm, beautiful, thin body? After all, he was gorgeous and didn't seem to have any apparent physical flaws. How could

I ever present myself to him on our wedding night with my loose stomach and stretch-marked hips? I was scared, embarrassed, and even ashamed of myself. I wanted to call off the wedding.

During one of our dates, Bill asked the dreaded question, "What's wrong with you tonight?"

With tears spilling out of my eyes, I presented him with the news that I didn't think I was good enough for him. "You have a beautiful body, and you've waited for God's best for you. How can I possibly be that? I'm fat and scarred from childbirth, and I don't want you to see me," I said.

With tears then pouring from his eyes, Bill took me into his arms and assured me that what he saw was beautiful. To him, I was a precious gift from God for whom he was willing to commit his love and life forever.

Even though he did his very best to convince me, neither the girl in the mirror nor I could believe that he would find me beautiful once he actually saw me on our wedding night.

The Big Reveal

The wedding day finally arrived. I had lost quite a bit of weight during the weeks before my wedding, and because of the extremely supportive undergarment I was wearing, I actually felt somewhat beautiful. The ceremony was simple and sweet, and at last, I was pronounced Mrs. Bill Cannon. We were both so excited, and Bill was the most handsome prince ever to live.

Throughout the day, I couldn't stop thinking about what was going to happen later that night. It wasn't the consummation of the marriage I was most anticipating, but the response I would see in Bill's eyes as he looked upon my naked body for the first time. I was almost sick about it.

After the final pictures were taken, the cake was cut, and the final goodbyes were said, Bill and I headed for our honeymoon suite. When we arrived in our room, there was a beautiful basket of fruit and candies along with a bottle of champagne sitting on the table. I desperately wanted to suck down the entire bottle to alleviate my nerves, but because my sweet virgin husband had never consumed more than a sip of a wine cooler, I didn't think it would be a blessing to him. Bravely, I plunged headstrong and sober into my fear.

The moment of truth finally arrived. With the room as dark as it could be without causing us to stumble, my wedding clothes were shed. The response that I was sure would come did not. My precious new husband received me gladly, and for a while, I allowed myself to be caught up in our romance, laying aside my disdain for my own flesh. God had truly granted me good things in the land of the living, as He had said he would.

Over the next several years of our marriage, my weight went up and down. I had two more children, and with each pregnancy, my weight went over 200 pounds. I gained and lost more pounds than I can count, but no matter what size I was, Bill always seemed excited to have me as his wife. Not one time did he mention my weight or ask me to change physically to be more pleasing to him. Even though I would sometimes verbally call him a liar, he maintained that I was truly beautiful to him, and nothing I thought would change that reality.

I could never accept it. I had learned in elementary school that only thin people were beautiful, and nobody could tell me any different.

Circumstances in my life were great. God had restored to me all the years that the enemy had stolen and had even blessed me with a dream-come-true marriage. Even so, I was still struggling with my reflection. I continued to find myself squeezing my thighs when I looked into the mirror to see what they would look like a few inches smaller. I still sucked in my gut and wished I could stay that thin when I released all my breath. I still even jumped up and down while totally naked just to watch my fat bounce around and then ridicule myself. The only difference between these times and those in my younger years was that the person I was looking at in the mirror had now grown to hate me so much that she actually wanted me dead.

Enemies All Around

No matter how much I tried to think the best about myself, my efforts would soon be destroyed. A simple trip to the grocery store would often leave me a pitiful mess. From the moment I got finished in the produce aisle, my mind would fill with negative self-talk. *Don't buy that. It will make you fatter than you are.* Or *Look at that lady, she's skinny but she's getting junk food. How unfair!* I couldn't simply be thankful for the provision to feed my family and leave it at that. It was a war, and I was the underdog.

The major onslaught wouldn't occur until I had finally reached the checkout stand. Having survived the mental anguish of food selection, I would be faced with an enemy line of fashion magazines. Every cover would have a beautifully thin woman on it, scantily clad, of course. The smiles on their faces were filled with mockery. It was almost as if they were saying to me, "Nah nah na nah nah, I'm skinny and you're not."

As if their mockery wasn't enough, the very articles within the magazines would validate the fact that being thin is the only way to be beautiful. Stories about women taking off weight and finally feeling sexy abounded. Even more stories relayed the method by which some celebrity had taken off weight and how you could, too. The unwritten messages to me were, "If you don't look like the women on these magazines, you are not beautiful," and "If you cannot lose weight, you are definitely not sexy."

The message that thinner is better wasn't verified for me only at the grocery store. It was everywhere. Watch people respond to those who've lost weight, and you'll understand what I mean. "Oh my gosh! Gloria, you look great. How did you take off the weight?" Or "You look beautiful, Sue. How much weight have you lost?" It's like someone has won a Nobel Peace Prize, or something, if they can manage to take off some weight, and those who have managed to achieve a smaller waistline deserve the red carpet. Always the silent message to me: "You have not lost weight. You are not beautiful, and you do not deserve our approval. You are not worth celebrating at your current size."

Some of the hardest moments were the times when I heard the messages at church. Of course no one was outright telling me that I was worthless because I wasn't thin. I know no one was even thinking that. But because even in the church, weight loss is so important, I would still hear the roars of approval when someone had been victorious on a diet. Even at times when I had lost a little bit of weight, it was instantly a cause for celebration. "Wow, have you been losing weight, Teasi?" This would immediately cause me to feel as if I were a better person in their eyes. The opposite was true, however, when I inevitably gained the weight back. The compliments would stop, and my self-esteem would plummet.

The comfort of my own home offered no sanctuary, either. Every time I would sit down and turn on the TV, commercials would come on to tell me I was a failure. "I joined so-and-so system and lost 40 pounds. Now my husband finally likes to show me off to his buddies. I've never felt prettier," some lucky gal would say. Another would proclaim, "This diet is a way to a better life. I used to be a fat pig, but now I'm a beautiful princess," or something like that. Several times an hour, I would hear the unsaid: "You are ugly because your butt is too big. You are not as pleasing to your husband as you would be if you were thinner. Poor you."

And I can't forget the years of programming I received at family gatherings. Thanksgiving, Christmas, birthdays, you name it. They all were a private emotional war zone for me when I wasn't looking my thinnest. It's not that anyone would ever openly ridicule me for being fat, but the thinner people in the family would get more compliments, by far. On both my mom's and dad's side, weight was always an issue. There were very skinny people all the way up to morbidly obese. The closer you were to the thin side, the more positive attention you got. It wasn't a malicious thing, it was just a thing.

And, of course, in addition to all of this, there was always my enemy in the mirror.

CHAPTER TWO

THE GIRL WHO CRIED WOLF

"There is no believing a liar,
Even when he speaks the truth."
-Aesop-

The first time I actively tried to lose weight was in sixth grade. I remember my method was to not eat anything but dinner. I don't know how long I did this, but I do know I was successful at losing some weight. People began to notice, and the positive feedback felt good. That was the start of a lifetime of dieting for me.

Of course this method of staying thin wasn't maintainable, and my weight went back up some. Through middle school, it just went up and down, but even my down was bigger than my friends'.

In high school, I was fairly active and was able to stay somewhat fit, but because of my build, I was always about 20 pounds heavier than my friends. I felt fat even though I wasn't.

Around this time I began giving myself mental pep talks. They would go something like this: *Teasi, you're doing great, but tomorrow, don't eat so much junk food. Your butt is getting a little big, and none of the guys are going to think you're cute.*

If I began to gain more weight, the thoughts would change to this: *You are such a fat pig. Why can't you just stay on the stupid diet? What is wrong with you? Why do you eat so much*?

It's funny how talking to yourself can actually seem like two different people having a conversation. At least this is how it was for me. There was the "trainer" me and the "client" me. The trainer always knew what should be done, and the client sometimes succeeded and sometimes failed. As I got older, it seems the client failed more and more.

By the time I was in my early 20s, I was usually 15 to 20 pounds heavier than I wanted to be. I began binge dieting and exercising episodes when I started to feel really bad about myself. This ultimately led to even more weight gain. I did several diets, and when I lost a little weight, it changed my whole perspective. Suddenly, life would be worth living again, until I gained the weight back.

When I gave my life to Jesus, my perspective changed somewhat. As I studied the Bible, I learned that Jesus is concerned with our hearts and not as concerned with our outward appearances. This was wonderful for my relationship with Him, but I knew it didn't change what people really thought. I was still surrounded with the proof that being thin was beautiful, so I couldn't let go of my desire to be thinner.

The Scale God

I guess you could say that my weight was an obsession with me. Even when my weight was down, I was thinking about it. It was a daily issue. By the end of each day, I could tell you every bite of food I put into my mouth and approximately how many calories I had consumed. If it was a good day, my "trainer" was easy on me before bed. But on the bad days, she would let me have it. I would fall asleep to her shouting, *You really blew it today, didn't you, Teasi? Tomorrow you should run three miles.*

Falling asleep that way didn't make waking up easy. My very first thoughts in the morning were about my weight. I would go straight to the scale, shed every possible piece of clothing, use the bathroom, and then step on the scale. Slowly, I would bow my head to see the results. If the number was favorable, I believed I deserved to have an okay day. If I had gained a pound or two, there was hell to pay. Not only for me, but often for those around me.

It was truly as if the scale were a god to me. My morning ritual was my homage to the god. Each morning, I would go to the god for it to tell me what I was worth that day. If I was losing weight, the god told me I was a good person and that I was becoming more beautiful. If I was gaining weight, the god told me the opposite, that I wasn't a good person and that I wasn't beautiful. I believed every word this false god said.

On the days that the god deemed me a miserable wretch, I wasn't a fun person to be around. The depression that would immediately set in seeped into every aspect of my life. I was able to function and experience temporary joy here and there, but deep inside, disappointment in myself was lurking. Many days, I would lack patience with my friends or family because of the pervading heaviness I felt in my heart.

My obsession with weight also caused me to be very judgmental of others. I couldn't help but compare my own condition to that of everyone around me. It's ugly to admit that a person's weight was the first thing I would take note of, but that's how it was. If the person I was looking at was thinner than I was, I would feel a bit of jealousy. If they were heavier than I was, I would think, *Well, at least I'm not that fat*, and this thought would bring me a bit of comfort. Being trapped in that type of superficiality is misery.

I was not only judgmental but would also rejoice in other people's calamity. Not all calamities, but if it was weight gain, inside, I would secretly rejoice. I can remember loving it when my friends would put on some weight. It was as if justice were finally being served. I knew that this thinking pattern was not pleasing to the Lord, but my mind was on autopilot. A mental stronghold had been developed in me, and it didn't want to let go.

Money down the Drain

I can't even begin to calculate all the money I spent on diets, weight loss supplements, videos, and books. I'm sure it is several thousands of dollars. Being trapped in my mental prison made me desperate to try any key holding promise of my release.

"I just know this is the key for me," I would say as I popped a new video in the VCR. "This new breathing technique has got to be the ticket." One week later, the video would be collecting dust.

Any vitamin promising an increased metabolism, I bought. Any product claiming that it would decrease your appetite, I tried. These would just make me irritable and sleepless, not thinner.

I paid for several weeks of a leading diet counseling and foods program on several different attempts at the diet. I paid for a prepackaged meal program on two different attempts on that diet. I paid the membership fees of a popular support group for several weeks, also on several different attempts.

The amount goes up God only knows how much when you start adding in all the diet books I purchased. I couldn't go through a bookstore without purchasing a diet book. It was as if I were magnetically attracted to that section. Once I was there, I would begin my hopeful search for the one book that held the answers for me.

The crazy thing is that each book I read had a different solution to my problem, and they would actually contradict each other. One book would say that eating too many carbohydrates was my problem and that I needed to eat mostly proteins and fats. The very next book I would read would say that I needed to eat mostly carbohydrates and that too much protein and fat were my problem. Another book would say it was all about the percentages of each food group that you eat, while yet another would say to let your appetite lead you and not to worry about counting anything. Talk about confusing!

Some say the definition of insanity is doing the same thing over and over and expecting a different result. Well, I was the living example of that. With each new product or book I purchased, my outlook got temporarily brighter as I believed I had found the answer. But not long after, when the victory hadn't come, I was back in a lower place than where I had started.

Don't Touch My Fat

The berating from the scale god each morning was bad. Feeling like an idiot for wasting so much money on diets wasn't good, either. But one thing that brought me down even further was how my weight issues were affecting me in the bedroom with my husband.

Like I said earlier, my husband has never expressed any problem with my physical appearance. In fact, he has always shown nothing but adoration and complete satisfaction in me, no matter what my weight. So, what's my problem, right? Well, the problem is that I always believed he was either a freak or a complete liar if he could be attracted to me. I did not understand how any man could find a fat woman sexy.

When we were first married, my husband and I enjoyed a very healthy sex life. But as more children came—and along with them, more pounds—what little desire I had to be seen naked was completely extinguished. Not only did I not want to be seen, I did not want to be felt. When my husband would simply reach over to hug me, I would instantly become aware of the fat on my body. I couldn't stand it. "Please don't touch my fat," I would say many times to Bill.

"I just want to hug you, though," he would reply, and I would feel like a total jerk.

Well, okay, I would think. *You can touch my wrists and ankles, and I think my shoulder blades are still firm and tone. Touch me there!* Sounds like the makings of a great love scene, doesn't it?

I knew in my head that my husband loved me and that he wanted to express his love, but my self-loathing kept me from receiving it. I would go through the motions, but my mind would be filled with thoughts of disgust regarding my own body instead of thoughts of love and thanksgiving for my precious husband.

My feelings of being a failure in this area of my life on top of all the others only made me more desperate to lose weight. I would fantasize in my head about how it would be when I could finally saunter into the bedroom wearing something tiny and strutting my stuff. With my new, thinner body, I would be worthy of my husband's love and could accept his touch. I would make grand plans for my next diet.

"I'm going to get all this weight off because my husband deserves to have a skinny wife," I would proclaim. The "trainer" in my head would quickly agree with my plan and add, *Yes, he deserves a thinner you. Don't fail again this time, dummy. If you do, you just make me sick.* The failure trap was set again.

Crying Out

Journal entry: June 28, 1997
I'm getting ready to go to sleep feeling overweight and defeated again. I am full of the knowledge of how to get my weight off. I know the key to success—among the many is giving my pain to God instead of food. I know I will never be skinny, and that's fine. I

don't need to be. I do want to be lean—fit. I want to be at a comfortable weight so that it is no longer an issue that keeps me bound in depression or feeling like a failure. I know what size I should be and can be. I want to be there, and I can do it with God's help and my own. I'm weary of the self-defeating cycle. I want off this horrible ride of falling asleep angry at myself and waking up to do what hurts me most: over eat and eat the wrong stuff too much. Lord, Jesus, I need your strength and mercy. I need Your forgiveness, and most desperately I need to see myself as You see me so that my focus will be healthy and godly. I don't want to be thinner for vain reasons. I want to feel good about my appearance, but mostly I want to be free of this self-mutilating process I'm in. I know I fall short in so many ways, but I come to You begging for mercy and strength.

That is one of many journal entries I've written in my life in which I pour out my self-disgust to God and ask Him to help me. In this entry, my heart cried out momentarily for the key to my freedom, but it would take almost 10 years for it to become crystal clear.

"I need to see myself as You see me," I included in my prayer, and that truly was what I needed. Sadly, at that time, my deepest desire was still that God would just help me lose the weight.

Journal Entry: February 13, 2001
I go to bed most every night regretting the eating choices I've made and feeling angry at myself. Then I make grand plans to do better—Plans I don't keep. I'm sick of this insanity, but apparently not enough to change it. I really, really, really want to figure out

what the heck keeps me in this horrible, self-defeating, hellish cycle. Why am I doing this? Why? Why? I feel like I'm drowning in the insanity of this. I want to be free.

Deep in my heart, the desperation was growing. My feelings of self-loathing were strengthened now by my oppressive sense of failure. I was a prisoner in a prison I could not see. My prayer reveals my confusion and hopelessness. I still believed that weight loss was the only answer, the only victory for me.

Journal Entry: November 16, 2002
Well, here I am again. I want to develop a plan of attack that will help me lose 15 pounds. I've lost quite a bit, but I need to lose these last few pounds. I need to continue to run five days a week and follow an eating plan correctly 98% of the time.

Journal Entry: May 20, 2003
Okay, I'm up again (on the scale) and wanting to be healthier and lose some weight. My goal is to lose 20 pounds. I think that would be a good weight for me. I need to set realistic goals. I'm not really sure how to eat. I'm confused, but I do know I love exercise. So, I'm going to say six days a week I need 30 minutes of aerobics. Then I need to make sure I'm drinking enough water.

Journal Entry: April 12, 2005 (still at it two years later)
Well, there are some things I want to do for myself. I don't really know how to make this time different than the rest of my attempts, but I've got to try. I've gotten myself up to a size 16-18. I'm not really happy at this

size. I want to be a 12. I know I will feel much more like myself at that size. I think a plan that will be good for me is to walk five days a week for 30 minutes or more and substitute meals for shakes and snack bars.

Feeling Like a Fool

Night after night for years, my "trainer" would beat me up, and night after night, the "client" me would make a plan of attack for the next day. I would desperately hope that I would follow through on the plan, but it got increasingly hard to believe myself. I was miserable.

To add to the misery, I was feeling like a total idiot to my friends and family. I used to talk about my weight a lot, and because of that, I was also talking about my dieting strategies. I would call my mom to tell her my new plan and how I was absolutely sure this time it would work and that I believed in myself. She would encourage me and tell me she believed in me, too, and then within weeks, I would have failed at the diet.

After a while, I began to wonder what my friends thought of me when I was discussing my new diets. I'm sure they got to a point where they were just feeling sorry for me. "Poor Teasi. She just can't get it together," they would probably be thinking. "All she needs to do is eat less and exercise more," they might have added.

Even though I knew I looked like a fool, it took me a long time to stop talking about my weight. My "trainer" even started adding this to my nightly pep talk: *We are not going to tell anyone about your new plan this time, okay?* she would insist. "Okay," I would agree. What was absolutely insane is that it was almost impossible for me to keep quiet about dieting because it had become such a habit for me to talk about it. I couldn't even succeed at keeping quiet about my dieting efforts, which only added to my feelings of self-loathing and failure.

I would sit up for hours, crying and trying to get my sweet husband to do something to help me out of the trap I was in. Because he was thin and had no issues with self-control, I knew he couldn't possibly understand what I was going through, but I was wishing he could figure out a way to help me. He did all he could. Poor guy. He listened, held me, paid for all my attempts to lose weight. He prayed for me, encouraged me, and told me nightly how beautiful I was to him. But none of his attempts helped.

I reached out to people at church who had ministries to overweight people, asking them for guidance. They would encourage me and give me great information about how to eat and be healthy. I wanted so badly to achieve weight loss success so that they would be proud of me and be able to rejoice. The only thing I achieved was a greater feeling of defeat and humiliation when I had to go back to them just as fat as ever. No one ever asked me why I wasn't losing weight, and they probably weren't even thinking about it, but in my mind, it was an elephant in the room that everyone was avoiding.

All the talking I did about dieting and the promises I made to my friends and family that I would "do it this time" left me feeling like quite an idiot. Of course the enemy loved this and took advantage of every one of my weak moments. He loved the fact that I was stuck in a failure trap, and he was hoping to watch me die there.

The Enemy in the Mirror Again

Feeling like a loser to my friends and family was difficult, but it was nothing compared to how I was beginning to feel about myself. My already low self-esteem and well-developed self-loathing began to worsen significantly.

With each diet I began and failed, my faith in myself weakened. During my nightly mental pep talks with the "trainer," I began to tell her to shut up. *It's no use anymore*, I would say. *I'm such a flippin' failure. There is no use trying a new diet anymore.*

I really had a hard time looking in the mirror. When I did, what I saw was an overweight failure, someone who was deeply flawed and without hope of change. My idea of success equaled weight loss, and I was unable to lose weight. This meant I was doomed to be a failure. I couldn't handle it. The depression I was beginning to feel was overpowering. I could not even imagine living my entire life looking the way I did, never losing the weight I needed to lose.

Nothing meant as much to me as losing weight. Even when people would compliment something else about me, I couldn't receive it. Someone might say, "Wow, Teasi, you're a really great mom," in my mind I would say, "Yeah, but I'm fat." Or they might say, "Thanks for your prayers. You are a real blessing to me." I would still think, "Yeah, but I'm fat." No other accomplishment or personality asset meant as much to me as being thin. I couldn't enjoy anything else about myself without first losing weight.

I prayed and prayed for answers. I confessed every sin I could imagine that might be responsible for me being fat. I asked people about deliverance ministry, thinking there might be some demonic influence keeping me overweight. Sometimes I went to the other extreme and wished there would be a demonic influence that would make me thin. Anorexia was something I longed for. I would have done anything to get weight off my body.

Even though I would go through the motions of life, nothing was truly enjoyable. On family vacations, on dates with my husband, at parties, anywhere, I was aware of my weight, and my disappointment in myself kept me from truly living.

Eventually, it got so bad that I began to contemplate suicide. Even though I had a wonderful husband, three beautiful children, a great family, and a wonderful church, life fell miserably short for me. I was dying inside, and I wanted to die for real. The pain I carried in my core because of my failure to lose weight was something I couldn't live with.

I remember sitting on my couch one day, wondering how painful it would be to drink a glass of bleach. I wondered what the reaction would be physically, because I didn't want it to be too traumatic for my precious children if they found me dead. The whole time I thought about it, I was shaking in tears. My heart felt like it was going to burst. I felt like I was suffocating and alone.

A Crack of Light

Thankfully, the Lord saved me from dying. By His strength and His strength alone, I dragged myself to the foot of the Cross. The pain of my self-loathing was my new motivation. I did not crawl to the Cross this time to find an answer to my weight-loss needs. I did not go to ask for a better metabolism or to ask the Lord to show me what diet to try next. I went to ask the Lord to take me home or change me completely. I no longer wanted to be trapped in self-loathing. I didn't want to read in the Bible that I was supposed to be living the more-than-abundant life but know that I was living much less. I wanted freedom. I needed freedom.

I had finally come to realize that what I had been doing all of my life was not working. I was even weary of thinking about weight. Though I still did not know exactly what I needed, I became willing to admit that weight loss might not be the plan God had for me. The thought made my stomach tight with anxiety, but I knew that if it was God's plan, He would give me the strength to deal with it.

All my efforts to achieve victory based on my definition of success had failed. It would take much healing for me to be able to understand and accept a new definition, but God's love was beginning to pour into the cracks of my heart, readying me to receive what was to come.

Journal Entry: April 10, 2006

I really don't have words, but I'm here again—wanting change—needing freedom and success—lasting success.

I pray today for healing in the deepest recesses of my heart and soul—healing in whatever wounded mechanism keeps me defeating myself. I give it to You, Lord. I love You and that's about all I do know.

I have no plan today except to hold desperately to You. I am Yours.

The Enemy of Our Souls

The Bible says that the Devil is roaming around like a lion looking for someone to devour (1 Peter 5:8). He almost got me. But for the grace of God, I could have easily become the enemy's prey. Still, he is targeting many others.

As I look around every day, I see countless victims of his lies. So many young girls and women believe that their beauty is directly related to their weight or looks. Even those who may not have weight issues deal with degrees of self-loathing because they do not measure up to the world's standard of beauty. We are all victims.

I see the Devil like a giant spider sitting atop his web. The web spans our nation from coast to coast and is made up of lies. The lies he spins have us trapped, and the only way out is to recognize the lies and choose to live in the truth.

It is important to be healthy. We should take care of our bodies. The Bible says that our bodies are the temple of God, so there is a reason to take care of them (2 Corinthians 6:16). If we have a weight issue that is a threat to our health, we should get help for that. Also, if food takes the place of the Father in our lives, it has become another god, and the Bible says we need to deal with that (Exodus 20:3).

But the obsession we have with weight loss in our generation is not of God. The value that is placed on being thin is not a value that has been given by the Father. It has been given by the Father of Lies. If the Devil can keep us consumed with the appearance of our flesh even part of the time, he has succeeded in keeping us from focusing on the appearance of our hearts, which is far more important to the Lord. The time we spend worrying about the size of our rear ends, or any other aspect of our appearance, is time we spend in prison. God wants us free.

I am thankful that my life was spared. I am even more thankful for the healing that the Father has and continues to so lovingly pour into my life. He has transformed my self-image and my definition of victory. It is my prayer that others will be set free, as well. If someone as bound in the enemy's lies as I was can be set free, so can you.

Throughout the rest of this book, I want to share with you the steps I took on my journey to freedom—steps that were taken as I began to see and understand the lies I had believed all of my life.

Not the Only Victim

One day I decided to randomly and anonymously poll several women in my Bible study at church. I wanted to see if they dealt with any feelings of inferiority as I did because of their physical appearances. Though the testing sample wasn't large, the answers, I believe, reveal the thoughts and feelings of a much larger group.

My findings weren't all that unexpected. Of the sample group, 71% said that their thoughts about themselves while looking in a mirror were negative more than half of the time. Some even admitted to having negative thoughts about themselves 80% of the time or more. Seventy percent of the women said they believe they would be more beautiful if they were thinner. Approximately 70% said that when they look at the women on the covers of fashion magazines, they wished they could look like that.

There were even women who admitted to staying home from church on occasion because of feeling fat or ugly. I have done that, too. Most admitted to talking about weight issues or physical appearance on a regular basis and thinking about it even more frequently.

Here are some of the specific thoughts these blood-bought daughters of God admitted to thinking when they look in the mirror:

> *"I hate my hair. I want a nose job. How can I be this old already? My hairline is receding."*
>
> *"I would be happier if my husband was happy with the way I look."*
>
> *"I would look better 20 pounds lighter."*
>
> *"I wish I could wear smaller clothes. I need to do more crunches today."*
>
> *"I wish my hair would do what everyone else's does. I wish my teeth were white and straight and beautiful. Ugh… I hate my smile and my teeth."*
>
> *"If I was thinner, if my teeth were straighter, if my hair was better, I would feel better about myself and I wouldn't be alone."*
>
> *"Why do I have to be so weak that I can't change myself or have the will power to just not overeat?"*
>
> *"I should not weigh this much."*

Every single woman had something she was not happy about with her physical appearance, and most were unhappy with their weight.

After looking at all their responses, it became clear to me that I wasn't the only one with an enemy in the mirror. Some may not have been as vicious as my own, but they were hurtful, nonetheless. It made me begin to wonder how many other women in the church, and in the world, look into the mirror and feel degrees of self-loathing. How much of our time is spent hating our own flesh? How have we become a society that places such enormous value on weight loss? Certainly, the enemy of our souls is behind this.

A Prayer for New Vision

Dearest Heavenly Father,

I love you. Thank You for loving me. Help me to begin to understand Your love more and more each day.

I confess that I have believed the lies of the enemy as it relates to my value as a person, and I have measured my beauty based upon the world's standard. In my mind, my beauty has been tied to the size of my body, and I know that this is not Your truth, Father, but what this world says. It is so hard not to fall into the trap of believing what I see on the television and in magazines. It is so hard to believe that my true worth and identity can be defined in any other way. But Father, I am willing to see it Your way now.

I want my eyes to be opened to Your truth. I want to see myself the way You see me, Father, because I know that You love me, and what You say will bring me life.

I'm not sure what this is going to take, but I'm willing to surrender my heart to You. Please heal me, Lord. Please change me, Lord. I need to be set free, and I know that it is for my freedom that You gave your life.

I choose life today. I choose You today. Open the eyes of my heart, Lord. Open the eyes of my heart. I want to see You. In the name of Jesus, Amen.

PART TWO

TRUTH TO THE RESCUE

CHAPTER THREE

WHO'S YOUR DADDY?

He loves me, He loves me not;
Who can really tell?
Things are hard to understand,
I thought I knew Him well.
Some days He feels close by me,
Some days He seems to flee.
Deep in my soul, the need to know,
For He is my Daddy.

"I'm taking you to Chicago this weekend," my husband adamantly insisted. "Even if you don't want to go, I know this is what you need."

I didn't want to go. I was depressed beyond anything I had ever known in my life because of self-loathing and a sense of deep failure. I had finally come to admit that weight loss might not ever come for me, and even though I had made a small step toward surrender, I was unable to feel even the slightest bit of hope for any true success in life. A large part of my heart felt dead.

Looking back at that time in my life reminds me of the tale of Snow White and the seven dwarfs. The beautiful princess is fooled by the evil queen and eats the poisoned apple. Snow White falls into a state that appears to be death, but she is not dead. The handsome prince arrives and kisses her on the lips, and she is awakened. What the evil queen had meant to destroy Snow White is turned to the good; Snow White discovers and experiences a new love.

For me, the evil queen was Satan. The poisoned apple I was tricked into eating was the lie that my beauty and value were equivalent to my weight and my inability to lose it.

When I ate the apple and chose to believe the lie, I experienced what looked like death: severe suicidal depression. The evil queen (Satan) was hoping I was really dead, but what was meant to destroy me ultimately led to my discovery and experience of a new love.

The reason my precious husband wanted to take me to Chicago was to attend a weekend seminar dealing with experiencing the Father's love. He had been listening to some tapes a dear friend of ours had loaned him, and he was absolutely certain this teaching was what I needed. It sounded like a bunch of sappy bologna to me, and I was cynical, to say the least. After all, I already knew God loved me, and it wasn't doing me any good.

Despite my pessimism, Bill loaded me into the car and drove eight hours north from our home in a last-ditch effort to resuscitate me. I know he was hurting and that watching me deal with so much inner pain was no picnic for him. He was trying his hardest to help. I can't thank him enough. If he hadn't pushed me to try that conference, I don't really know where I'd be.

Bless Me…I Dare You!

As the conference began, we found our seats. The room was filled with what appeared to be people from all different planets. When you leave the comfort of your home church and venture out into the land of a conference, you never know what you're going to see. I was getting an eye full.

In different areas around the room were men, women, and children holding banners, which they promptly began to swing around when the worship music started. Even though they seemed totally comfortable with this activity, it was my first experience with it. I knew in my heart that these were

God's children and that He was thrilled and blessed by their expression of love for Him. I, however, was not thrilled. I was irritated.

I sat with my arms crossed tightly across my chest while worshippers of every kind (including a lady who appeared to be doing a pole dance for the Lord) entered into the presence of God right in front of me. *This is so stupid,* I thought. *Get me out of here. This isn't going to do any good.* I had made up my mind before the conference even started that nothing was going to change me, and I doubted God was even there. But just in case God decided to show up after the worship, I stayed.

Finally, the keynote speaker walked to the front of the room. He was a tall man, seemingly normal, but his name was Jack Frost. *Is this for real?* I thought. *Who has a name like Jack Frost? Are we at the North Pole, or something?* Every thought that went through my mind was soaking with sarcasm. Soon I began daring God to show up. *You better show up and say something to me. Don't you know I want to die? I demand to hear a voice this time. I mean, make it loud and clear. Got it?* Obviously, I wasn't being humble or teachable at that point.

Mr. Frost finally began to tell his story. He told of how he had been a hardened but extremely successful sea captain and had been raised by a very authoritarian father who had belittled him often. He told many amazing sea stories that I have to admit were fascinating, but all the while, I was thinking to myself, *This isn't working. I'm feeling nothing.* I kept giving Bill quick glances, making sure he could see the irritation in my eyes.

I continued to listen while Jack told his story. Even though I wasn't feeling anything in my heart at that point, this man most assuredly was. I could sense that what he had was genuine, and the life he claimed to be experiencing sounded great. He was passionate and transparent. I appreciated this transparency. I needed it. A superficial discussion would have surely pounded the nails into my coffin.

The first session came to a close, and some soft music began to fill the room. Jack began to say some prayers over the whole group, and people all around began to weep. People were on the floor in the front of the room, crying their guts out. It seemed God was really moving on those people. *What about me?* I thought. I was getting angry. *I'm here to get Your help, don't Ya know?* Underneath the angry cries was a feeling of desperation. I knew that if I didn't hear from God here, there truly was nothing left for me.

Bill could see my desperation. I looked at him and told him that I was feeling nothing. "God is not answering me," I told him. "This isn't working." With that, Bill decided to go get Jack Frost himself to come pray over me. Surely that would help.

Jack came over and sat by me. I looked him straight in the eyes and said, "I don't feel anything. I like what you're saying, but I don't feel anything."

He wasn't shaken. He replied something like, "It's okay that you don't feel anything. That doesn't make the truth not true. The Father loves you and longs for you to experience His love." He then prayed a prayer for me. I was hoping that while he prayed, I would begin to shake or fall down or experience some miraculous change in my pulse, anything. But I felt nothing.

Once he finished praying, Jack walked away. I sat there wondering if there was any hope for me. *Am I already dead?* I thought. Fortunately, there were several sessions of the conference yet to come.

Feeling It a Little

Although my help did not come the way I had demanded it to, slowly but surely, light began to shine on the darkness in my soul. I didn't realize it at the time, but the truths I was learning at that conference, delivered by the sea captain with the odd name, were the seeds that would rather quickly transform my life.

The main message of that weekend was that our Heavenly Father loves us and wants us to experience His love. It seemed like a no-brainer to me, and I honestly believed I already had a grasp on that concept. I truly did not.

God says in His word that He longs for us to experientially know and believe in the love that He has for us because He is love (1 John 4:16). Many times we may think we know and believe God loves us, but it may simply be head knowledge and not experience. This is what I discovered was my issue.

All of my Christian life, I had known God loved me because the Bible says He does. I understood that it must have taken love for Him to send His only Son to die for me. I could see the evidence of His love in my life in many ways, such as my second chance in marriage, fulfillment of my physical needs, the blessing of friends, and so on. But there was a blockage in my heart keeping me from actually feeling or experiencing His love for me, and because of that, I was not reaping the full benefits of the love, and the resulting void was a home for my growing depression and self-loathing.

I eventually learned that there were several blockages in my heart were keeping me from experiencing God's love. The Bible says in John 7:38, "He who believes in Me, as the scripture has said, out of his heart will flow rivers of living water." The next verse explains that the living water is actually the Holy Spirit, whose fruit is love, joy, peace, patience, kindness, goodness, gentleness, and self-control. None of this was flowing from my heart. Yes, there were times in my life that I felt a bit of joy or was patient with my children, but nothing could be described as flowing from my heart except sadness and even bitterness.

Because of His amazing mercy, the Lord began to reveal to me the biggest cause of the blockage in my heart. He showed me that I had an incorrect view of the Father. I didn't really believe that I had a wrong view of the Father; after all, I believed everything that I read about Him in His word. I knew He was good and mighty. I believed He wanted good things for me.

The truth is, if I had genuinely believed all of these things in my heart, I would never have become the mess that I was.

An Unfair Rap

"You're grounded until your attitude changes or Christ returns, whichever comes first," my mom said to me at times during my childhood. You see, I was prone to exhibiting a bad attitude. I was the typical child who didn't like to do her chores or play with her younger siblings, and unfortunately, I wasn't afraid to show my true emotions.

Having a good attitude in life is important. After all, attitude has the power to change our perspective in any given situation. The lesson my parents were trying to teach me was a good one, and I'm thankful they were so diligent in enforcing it. The problem was that I took it a little too hard.

When I was grounded for my attitude, I would typically be sent to my room. I was anything but a joy to be around with all my grumbling and complaining, so after school, I would spend time in my room until dinner. After dinner, I would go back to my room. As soon as I could humble myself and exhibit a good attitude, my grounding would be over. Then I could return to full fellowship with the family. The length of my grounding was basically up to me. Unfortunately, my childish pride got the best of me. It wasn't uncommon for me to go tell my parents I had learned my lesson, only to roll my eyes yet again. Back into the room I would go.

I applaud my parents for their consistency and tenacity. They truly did love me and wanted to see my attitude problems disappear. They were so patient with me. Looking back, however, I can see a behavioral pattern that eventually affected my relationship with God as my Father.

The pattern was this: I would exhibit some manifestation of a bad attitude, my mom or dad would lovingly yet firmly discuss why my attitude was wrong and what I should do to make it right, and then I would be removed from fellowship with my family for a period of time. Eventually, relationship would be restored when I could exhibit a good attitude. Sounds pretty normal, huh?

Spring forward into my adult years. I still carried with me a tendency to have a bad attitude at times. Maybe I didn't like my job, or the kids were driving me crazy, or there wasn't enough money in my bank account; the scenarios could be endless. I would pray about my problems, asking God for His help, knowing in my head that He loves me. My heart was, however, unable to receive or accept the Father's love because, ingrained in my perception, was the belief that to be in a right relationship with Him, my attitude needed to be good. And I doubted that my attitude would ever be good enough.

I didn't realize it, but all my Christian life, I had been attributing a characteristic to our Heavenly Father that He didn't deserve. I lived my life as if God were expecting me to get my attitude right before He could bless me or truly answer my prayers. I lived my life as if I needed to perform in some way to earn His love. Even though what my parents had tried to teach me was a good lesson, in my heart, I had transferred their painstaking efforts to the Father when I left their home. Now it had become God's job to "ground me" until my attitude changed or Christ returned.

This may seem like a small misconception of Father God, but it was a major blockage for me. I was unable to truly believe and receive the absolute unconditional love He longed to pour upon me. In effect, I was holding my hand up in refusal of the very thing He was trying to give, the very thing that could change my attitude and completely transform my life.

Once I began to see what I had been doing to God, treating Him in a way He didn't deserve, I immediately began to feel new life rush into me. As I looked at the Word, His true nature and heart toward me started to become clearer than ever before. I'm sure God was thrilled to have His rap sheet expunged.

Other Misconceptions

I've always believed that God designed families to be a safe place in which children can learn about Him and His true nature and that our parents, especially our fathers, are intended to lovingly model the relationship we would one day grow to have with our Heavenly Father. But, as we all know, since the fall of man, God's perfect plan has not been carried out. No parents have been perfect, and even the best fathers are nowhere near as amazing as Father God is.

Depending on what kind of a father (or mother) we have as children, I believe, it's possible to attribute some of their characteristics to Father God. Just as I believed deep in my mind that God was waiting on me to get my attitude right before He could truly bless me, others may have developed a wrong view of God as a result of their upbringing.

I can imagine the child who has a very authoritarian father. The father comes home from work each day tired and irritated. He expects dinner on the table immediately, and he wants his children to be seen and not heard. He expects immediate obedience and will tolerate no silliness. If the child is brave enough to discuss anything about her life with her father at the table, she'd better make sure it is what he wants to hear. The grades had better be good. The team had better have won. This father doesn't want to hear it if it isn't perfect. After all, he is working very hard to afford his daughter the privileges she has, and not doing everything perfectly is interpreted as a lack of appreciation.

Then I think of this child as an adult. All of her life, she has been striving to please her earthly father. When she performed well for her dad, he was happy with her. When she failed, he was displeased and he withdrew his love. I can see how this grown woman may now be the one who feels she must volunteer for every ministry need that arises in her church. If the nursery needs help, she will be there. If the bathrooms need to be cleaned, she's on it. She might believe she needs to pray more, study the Bible more, and do more and more and more to please God. In her heart, she may believe she has to earn God's love through performance just as she had to earn her dad's. But it's not true. This misconception of the Father could keep her from accepting the true, unconditional love He is lavishing upon her.

I can also imagine a child with a passive father. This father is present in the home and doesn't demand much. In fact, he doesn't seem to demand anything. He comes home from work and sits down to watch TV. He wants dinner in the living room so he won't miss the big game. When his little girl walks in, he smiles at her and says a few words but does not engage in any meaningful conversation with her. Mom takes care of this little girl's emotional needs and does most of the talking in the family, while dad just seems like he's along for the ride, silent and emotionless.

I wonder if this child will grow to become a woman who keeps her relationship with Father God intellectual because of what she is used to with her earthly father. Perhaps she will assent to the truth of the Word, but any emotional displays brought on by moves of the Holy Spirit, she may see as unnatural or uncomfortable. Because God longs for us to experience His love, and experiencing His love involves our emotions, this woman's misconceptions could hinder her ability to receive His love.

My heart hurts even more when I think of a child whose father is abusive. When he comes home, his children will run, not to greet him, but to hide. He is probably drunk and is definitely a threat. Some days he is sober and seems like a decent guy. As soon as this little girl begins to trust her daddy, he comes home drunk again and slugs her in the mouth. Then he threatens to beat her mom and her little sister. She does everything she can to try to stop him from hurting them, including succumbing to his desire to touch her in inappropriate ways.

I can see this girl growing up to be a woman with deep wounds. She may not even be able to relate to God as the Father at all. Why should she? She will accept her salvation from Jesus. He is her big brother, the one who protects her from a Father who is unpredictable and at times cruel. The way her earthly father treated her all of her life might cause her to unconsciously believe God isn't trustworthy either. Though they seem very real, the lies she believes about our Heavenly Father are the very tools that I could see the enemy using to keep her lost and afraid.

There are so many other misconceptions we may have about Father God. Even if our parents were loving and represented Him well, there may be unhealthy and inappropriate significant adults in our lives who taint our perceptions. There might also be unfortunate experiences with legalistic and harsh churches. Wounds from the people in a church might cause us to attribute their characteristics to God.

No matter where we may have picked up the tainted lenses through which we see our Heavenly Father, we need Him to reveal to us His true nature. He longs to be known for who He really is. All we need to do is ask.

"Ask, and it shall be given to you; seek, and you shall find; knock, and it will be opened to you." (Mathew 7:7)

Who Our Heavenly Daddy Really Is

After I began to see that my perception of Father God was faulty, my heart became open to seeing Him in new ways. Scriptures I had read time and time again began to have deeper meaning, a life-giving meaning. I felt almost foolish for having missed these truths for so many years, but I was thankful to be seeing new things about this heavenly Daddy of mine because I needed Him so desperately.

When I began to think honestly about my perception of the individual members of the Trinity, it had looked like this:

Jesus—He is my loving savior, the one who allowed Himself to be sacrificed on my behalf. He is a humble, gentle man who adored children and healed the sick. I like this guy. I can trust Him.

Holy Spirit—He is the spirit sent by my friend Jesus after He went to be with the Father. He is my comforter and gives me wisdom in times of need. He is safe, and I like him.

The Father—He is the grand disciplinarian. He sits on His throne, shaking His head in disbelief as his children everywhere disappoint Him. If it were not for Jesus begging Him to have mercy on us, we'd all be toast. Sometimes He is happy with me, and I like it when He is, but when He's not, watch out!

I suspect many of us would admit to having similar ideas of the godhead. But when we take a closer look at what the Bible really says, it blows this theory out of the water.

Look at the life of Jesus, the one we all would admit is kind and safe. What do we see Him doing and saying?

"Most assuredly, I say to you, the Son can do nothing of Himself, but what he sees the Father do; for whatever He does, the Son also does in like manner. For the Father loves the Son, and shows Him all things that He Himself does..." (John 5:19–20)

And he says, *"For I have not spoken on my own authority; but the Father who sent Me gave Me a command, what I should say and what I should speak. And I know that His command is everlasting life. Therefore, whatever I speak, just as the Father has told Me, so I speak." (John 12:49–50)*

Jesus is saying in these scriptures that He doesn't do or say anything but what He sees the Father doing. As a matter of fact, He says that He doesn't do anything of His own initiative, only what the Father taught him (John 8:28, 38). He was following the Father's example.

So, what do we see Jesus doing? Throughout the gospels, we see Him hanging out with sinners, healing the sick, forgiving adulterers, loving on lepers, telling people to love their enemies, calming stormy seas. All of this, He did on cue from His Father. He was demonstrating the heart of mercy, compassion, and kindness toward sinners and people who didn't look like they deserved it.

The story that really got to me was this:

"Jesus, knowing that the Father had given all things into His hands, and that He had come from God, and was going to God, rose from supper, and laid aside His garments, took a towel and girded Himself. After that, He poured water into a basin and began to wash the disciples' feet, and to wipe them with the towel with which he was girded." (John 13:3–5)

The deep truth in this scene was very powerful to me, even life changing. If Jesus says when we see Him, we see the Father (John 14:9), what we are seeing in this scene is a representation of Father God's desire to sit at our feet and wipe away the filth. What Jesus was washing off of the disciples' feet was a mixture of dirt and animal feces. I was blown away and completely undone by the image of my Heavenly Father sitting at my feet, looking up at me—*up* at me—lovingly wiping away the dirt and grime that I had picked up as I walked through life. Suddenly, this disciplinarian God became someone altogether different in my mind. I saw a gentle Daddy who was saying, "Come here, my sweet girl. Let Daddy wash away the filth and the pain. Will you let me wash your feet?" As I allowed the Holy Spirit to transfer this truth from my head to my heart, I began to experience the Father's love in a completely new way. The truth of Daddy's love, of His true heart toward me, poured over me like warm oil.

Jesus said, "I am the way, the truth, and the life. No one comes to the Father except through me" (John 14:6). I was beginning to understand this statement more clearly than ever before. If there is a "way," there must be a place to get to, a destination. Jesus is saying that He is the way to the Father. He wants us to look at His life and see the heart of the Father so that we will climb back into Daddy's lap and be reconciled to Him. The purpose of Jesus' life was not only to ensure us eternal salvation from hell after death but to restore us to the heart of Father God in life. If we stop short of the full benefit of Christ's life, we are missing the point.

For the first time in my life, I was beginning to know the truth about my Heavenly Father, and as the Bible says, it's the truth that sets us free (John 8:32).

The Stage Is Set

Picture in your mind a vase that has a little bit of water in it. On top of the water are several small ping pong balls and other lightweight objects. If someone takes another pitcher of water and begins to pour water over the ping pong balls into the vase, the water level will rise. Eventually, some of the balls will be displaced, and, once the vase becomes filled to the top, water will begin to pour out the top of the vase. Got the picture?

Now, think of the vase as our hearts. The little bit of water that is in the vase represents the love of God that is given to us at the time of our salvation. We are instantly given the Holy Spirit, and in our Spirit man, we are perfected, the water is pure. But what about the ping pong balls?

The ping pong balls represent all our misconceptions, wounds, sins, and other things that block the water level from rising. In other words, they block our ability to live by the Spirit. They actually keep us from experiencing the things the Bible says we should be experiencing.

These ping pong balls also represent our habits of thought and our behaviors that have built up over a life time. The feelings of guilt and shame we may experience as a result of these add to the blockage. So what do we do about it? Nothing.

Now remember the other pitcher of water. Let this represent Father God's love. He is the other person waiting to pour the water (His love) over the ping pong balls (our wounds, etc.). If we will allow Him to do this, the water level within us will rise. We will begin to experience more of the love He placed deep within us at salvation, and as the water level rises, the ping pong balls will begin to be displaced. If we continue to allow Him to pour His love into us, eventually, we will become so full that His love will overflow out of us. This is what I believe is meant by the promise Jesus gives in the book of John: *"He who believes in Me, as the scripture has said, out of his heart will flow rivers of living water" (John 7:38).*

If we believe in Him "as the scripture has said." What does it say? It says that He, Jesus, is the direct representation of the Father's heart. If we believe it, and receive it, then out of our hearts will flow rivers of living water. Out of our hearts will flow love, joy, peace, patience, kindness, etc. It will just happen. We don't have to do anything but believe and receive! Amazing.

This revelation was the beginning of freedom for me. The stage was set for what was to come. My self-loathing did not disappear automatically; there was still more healing to come. But I understand now that there was no possible way for me to love myself without receiving the Father's true, unconditional love first. I am unable to love myself if I don't understand that I am worthy to be loved. Only the Father could show me that. For the first time, I was allowing Him to.

A Healing Prayer

Precious Heavenly Father,

Oh, Father, I can't believe how I have misjudged You. All these years, the lies I have believed about Your true heart have kept me from feeling the unconditional love You have desired to give. Please forgive me for that, Father. I did not understand the truth, but now I am beginning to see.

Please continue to open my eyes to the ways I have misperceived You. I want to trust you completely and to experience Your love. Fill me from head to toe. Fill me to overflowing with Your unconditional love.

From this day forward, I put upon my eyes new lenses through which to see Your true nature. I want to know You more. When I read Your Word now, it will not be out of religious duty, but to understand more clearly the heart of a Daddy who adores me. I need to know everything about You.

Father, let Your love so fill my heart that all other healing I may need can occur. I understand that I cannot love myself or others unless I am first filled with Your amazing love for me. I accept that and embrace that truth. Fill me up, Father. Fill me up.

I thank you, precious Lord Jesus, for showing me the heart of the Father in all that You did while You were on earth. Thank You for being the way to Him. Thank You for showing us how to climb back into Daddy's lap. Thank You for dying for my sins. Thank You for the complete work You did on the Cross. You are amazing.

I love You. I embrace the life You have for me. I embrace change. I embrace healing.

In Jesus' Precious Name,

Amen

CHAPTER FOUR

AN ORPHAN'S HEART

One friend comes and takes my doll, cheerfully sitting to play
My heart rate soars, my stomach's a knot
Hey! That belongs to me.
Another comes and takes my role, making the audience laugh
The tears roll down, my stomach's a knot
Hey! That belongs to me.
Again one comes and takes the guys, walking around so thin
The anger builds, my stomach's a knot
Hey! That belongs to me.
Another friend comes and takes the stage,
teaching the Word of God
Hopelessness invades, my stomach's a knot
Hey! That belongs to me.
The Father comes and takes my heart,
gently pouring in His love
Jealousy leaves, inheritance comes
Yes! That belongs to me.

Gently, I set the needle of my record player down onto my overplayed *Grease* soundtrack. Olivia Newton John begins to sing the anthem of my life once again, and I do my best to sing along—"Hopelessly Devoted to You." Tears stream down my cheeks as I watch myself cry in the mirror. There is no one to whom I am singing; it is just fun to watch myself cry. Self-pity is a comfortable garment for me.

I can remember this scene occurring many times in my childhood and preteen years. It seems ludicrous, but I was actually happy when I was sad. I enjoyed feeling sorry for myself and trying to get others to feel sorry for me, too. My parents called me Bette Davis quite often because of my dramatic flair, but what was growing inside of me was much darker. Seeds of jealousy and insecurity were sprouting, and the fruit they produced only added to my self-rejection.

I can remember it starting at such a young age—being jealous of what my friends had. Because we didn't have a lot of money when I was growing up, there was a lot for me to be jealous of. Of course, that doesn't make it right, but deep inside of me, I felt like I had been dealt the short end of the stick. Life just wasn't fair in my mind, and because of that, I was bitter.

I was also very possessive of my friends. From first grade until sixth, I had only one friend, and I loved her very much. We had lots of fun together and got along well, until she decided to do something with someone other than me. The fury that would spew out of me was startling. "How dare you go and spend the night with Lee Ann. I would never do that to you. How can you spend the night with someone other than me?" My poor friend wouldn't really know how to deal with me. She couldn't help it that she had other friends.

It didn't get much better in middle school. I added a few other friends to my life, but up until ninth grade, I still considered only the one girl my best friend. I tried very hard to allow her to have a life, but it was difficult. When other people asked her to go to their parties or sit with them at lunch, I was filled with jealousy. I was jealous not only of her time, but also of her. She was so skinny. She was beautiful and talented. I wanted to be those things. I wanted to fit into clothes like she did. I wanted a house like her family had. I wanted the boys to like me, too. I wanted, I wanted, I wanted.

When I was 15, my family moved from Indiana to California. Even though it was a tearful goodbye, I'm sure that somewhere deep inside, my friend was feeling happy about her new breathing room. It was hard for me to leave, but it didn't take long for me to meet my new best friend, another skinny and beautiful girl.

In high school I became aware that it was socially unacceptable to be a possessive jerk with your friends, so I learned how to keep my true feelings inside. When my friend wanted to do things with other people, I would act like it wasn't bothering me, but inside I would deal with great amounts of rejection and bitterness. I didn't want to lose her friendship because she was a fun person, but it was very hard for me. She was funny, she was beautiful, she got the lead role in our school plays, the boys loved her, and I was jealous. I wanted all of that. I wanted, I wanted, I wanted.

Thou Shalt Not Covet

In college I met a new best friend. She was thin and beautiful, and, of course, I was jealous. I hated it when she would do things with other people, and sometimes I made the mistake of letting her know. I'm sure she thought I was a basket case, because sometimes the pain I felt was so deep that I would cry. Just imagine a 20-year-old woman crying because her friend went to dinner with someone else. Kind of pathetic!

Because of God's amazing grace and goodness, my friend and I both accepted Christ around the same time and even got baptized together. Our friendship continued to grow as we fell in love with Jesus and accepted His forgiveness for all of our sins. As I began to study the Bible, I learned along the way that jealousy is not pleasing to the Lord. I knew that it was wrong to covet what someone else has, but I couldn't stop myself.

I can remember being at church and seeing people talking to my friend across the room. *Why do they think she is so great?* I would think to myself. *What's wrong with me? Why don't they want to talk to me?* Bitterness would rise up within me, and before I knew it, I would be having a decent pity party. Because I knew this was not pleasing to the Lord, I would feel even more miserable about myself. I hated the feelings I had inside, but I didn't know what to do about it.

My friend eventually moved to another church. I don't blame her. It couldn't have been fun seeing me glaring at her when she was simply trying to engage in fellowship with the brethren. When we were attending the same church, things often became a competition. Not to her, of course; just to me. Even so, I'm sure she could sense it.

As the years went by, I learned more and more about what the Bible says is pleasing to God. I learned that He loves a faithful servant, so I faithfully served in my church. I learned that He loved a cheerful giver, so I cheerfully gave my tithes and offerings. I knew that He wanted us to diligently study the His word, so I did Bible study upon Bible study. I did all the things I thought a good Christian should do. The problem was that my motives were all wrong.

It is almost embarrassing to admit, but over the years, there have been times when my service at church wasn't totally about pleasing God or loving others. At times, it was all about me. It's not that I was consciously aware of this, but deep within my heart, my motive was that I wanted *people* to think I was a great servant. I wanted *people* to think I was a very godly woman. I wanted everyone to approve of me and sing my praises. My need for the approval of man was deep, and when I didn't think I was getting it, I became more and more bitter inside.

Because I needed the approval of man so desperately, everything seemed like a competition to me in my mind. I would watch other members of the church who seemed to be getting the praise and admiration of my pastor, and I would mentally measure myself up to them. *I've been here since this place was a small Bible study*, I would think to myself. *Why the heck is she getting so much attention?* Or *She's only served in this nursery for one month, and she's already being put in charge. What about me? I'm in here every Sunday.*

My jealousy easily turned into bitterness, which then turned into resentment, judgment, condemnation, and many other dark motivations. To add to my torment, everyone around me seemed to be just fine. I could see that my church family was growing. People were getting saved, and ministries were being birthed. I was unable to fully rejoice because my perspective was so twisted. I was hurting so desperately inside, but my resentment kept me in pride, which kept me from facing my own sin.

Because I had the Holy Spirit inside me, my heart was terribly grieved by the ungodly thoughts that continually went through my mind. I didn't want to be so jealous. I hated being bitter. Even so, I felt desperately trapped in my mental strongholds. On top of hating my body, I had developed an even deeper hatred for my mind. All of this added to my suicidal depression. Thankfully, the weight of this ungodly burden was eventually lifted off of me by the Father.

The Bitter Sister

At that conference my husband had carted me to in Chicago, the Father was able to begin peeling yet another layer of blindness off my spiritual eyes. I had begun to experience the Father's love like never before as a result of seeing how I had misperceived Him in the past, and I was beginning to have hope for the first time in a long while. But God had more in store for me.

During one of the last sessions of the weekend, I heard a teaching that opened the door to a new depth of healing. Though the basis of the teaching was a story I had read on many occasions, the Father supernaturally made the words new and powerful to me this time. It was the story of the prodigal son:

And [the prodigal son] arose and came to his father. But when he was still a great way off, his father saw him and had compassion, and ran and fell on his neck and kissed him. And the son said to him, "Father, I have sinned against heaven and in your sight, and am no longer worthy to be called your son." But the father said to his servants, "Bring out the best robe and put it on him, and put a ring on his hand and sandals on his feet. And bring the fatted calf here and kill it, and let us eat and be merry; for this my son was dead and is alive again; he was lost and is found." And they began to be merry.

Now his older son was in the field. And as he came and drew near to the house, he heard music and dancing. So he called one of the servants and asked what these things meant. And he said to him, "Your brother has come, and because he has received him save and sound, your father has killed the fatted calf." But he was angry and would not go in. Therefore his father came out and pleaded with him. So he answered and said to his father, "Lo, these many years I have been serving you; I never transgressed your commandment at any time; and yet you never gave me a young goat, that I might make merry with my friends. But as soon as this son of yours came, who has devoured your livelihood with harlots, you killed the fatted calf for him." And he said to him, "Son, you are always with me, and all that I have is yours. It was right that we should make merry and be glad, for your brother was dead and is alive again, and was lost and is found." (Luke 15:20–31)

The teaching that followed was not the typical story of sinners—of backslidden Christians returning to the loving arms of a merciful God. That story is wonderful, but the focal point of this lesson was the other brother— the one who had never gone. As I read over the words again, I couldn't help but see myself in that older, bitter brother. It was not a pleasant revelation.

As I thought about the story, I could just hear what was going through the older brother's mind, because it is what often went through mine: "You've got to be kidding! What about me?"

The older brother was jealous, just as I had been at times throughout my life. He had been doing all the right things. He worked for his father and obeyed him, but his motives were wrong. Maybe this older brother had been working all his life for the approval of man, as I had. Maybe he had served his father out of fear of failure or losing his father's love. Whatever his motives, they weren't right, because if they had been, his reaction to this party would have been completely different.

The bitter brother says to his father, "You have never given *me* a kid that I might be merry with *my* friends, but when this son of yours came…" This son of yours. I can hear the sarcasm in his words. Hidden behind the resentment is a sad truth: The older brother had not been experiencing a healthy relationship with his father. He saw his younger brother, but not himself, as his father's son. He lived his life as if he were a servant and therefore had to fight for everything he got. He was jealous when his brother's life was celebrated because he didn't believe his *own* life was celebrated.

It hit me that what I was seeing in this story was the perfect description of me. I was the bitter older sister, jealous of the party others were having.

The Father's Reply

When the father said to the older brother, "Son, you are always with me, and all that I have is yours," I can just imagine the gentle look the father must have had on his face: eyes pleading with his son to believe him. I'm certain his words were said with kindness and love.

"My child," he said. These two words reveal that the relationship problem wasn't a result of the father's view of his son. No, it was the son's view of the father that was the root of the pain.

Next, the father said, "all that is mine is yours." Wow! He is basically saying, "Son, I love you. There is nothing for you to be jealous about, because all that I have is yours. You have an inheritance, too."

The older brother must not have believed in his heart that he was his father's son. He was living as if he was an orphan with no inheritance and no home, feeling sorry for himself for no *real* reason. This is exactly how I had been living. The reason I would find myself jealous of others' things and accomplishments was that I didn't believe I had anything of my own coming to me. I had always felt that I had to perform in some way to earn Father God's love, and I lived like He had an inheritance and blessings for all of his children except me. I was, in my heart, a spiritual orphan resentful of anyone who seemed to be a biological child.

As I began to see myself in this bitter brother and began to see that I was living as if I had no place in God's kingdom—as if I weren't really His child—the door to my heart opened a little further, allowing more healing to begin. It was not easy to admit that much of the disappointment in my life had been my own fault.

The Bible tells us:

> *For as many who are led by the Spirit of God, these are sons of God. For you did not receive the spirit of bondage again to fear, but you received the Spirit of adoption by whom we cry out, "Abba, Father." The Spirit Himself bears witness with our spirit that we*

are children of God, and if children, then heirs—heirs of God and joint heirs with Christ, if indeed we suffer with Him, that we may also be glorified together. For I consider that the sufferings of this present time are not worthy to be compared with the glory which shall be revealed in us. (Romans 8:14–18)

This tells us that if we are being led by the Holy Spirit, which we have in us when we accept Jesus as our Lord and Savior, then we are God's children. All of us. God does not have any stepchildren or grandchildren. We all have our own inheritance. We are joint heirs with Jesus Himself.

As I began to let these words penetrate my heart like never before, I became painfully aware of all the years I hadn't considered myself a true child of God. In my mind, I had known I was His, but in my life, I had been living as if I weren't. I didn't really understand why I had been living this way all my life, until God lovingly began to show me.

From the Womb

When my mother was 18 years old, she left home because her evil stepfather basically kicked her out. He not only kicked her out, but greedily took the money my grandma had been saving to send my mom to college and bought himself a Cadillac with it. My mom was on her own for the first time.

She was soon introduced to an older man who seemed to care for her. She was lost and afraid and took him at his word. It did not take long for her to become pregnant with me. She was 19 years old, unwed, and pregnant. To make matters worse, the man she thought she loved didn't feel the same for her. Her life became filled with uncertainty. Not a very good time to become a mommy.

When my mom finally figured out she wasn't in a happy relationship, she set out on her own again. She was out in the world with a baby growing inside her. I can't even imagine the feelings of total insecurity she must have been plagued with. She couldn't go home. There seemed to be no refuge for her.

Sometimes I wonder what I might have picked up on in the womb. I know some studies have concluded that, in some ways, babies who are played classical music before birth are more intelligent. Many parents can't wait to learn the gender of their babies before birth so they can begin to call the babies by name. They believe that the babies can hear them and will identify their voices.

All of this is wonderful for the baby who is conceived in a happy home. But think of the baby who is not. Does she feel her mother's stress? Does she sense that she isn't coming at a convenient time? If a baby responds to sweet and comforting sounds in the womb, wouldn't she also respond to the sound of profane yelling and threats? I wonder if the baby can sense that the mother has no clue what she is going to do with the little life growing inside of her. I wonder, because that is how my life started out.

At such a young age, my mom was a strong woman, determined to protect the little life she now was responsible for. I can't imagine how difficult it must have been for her, all alone at the age of 20 with a baby girl. From what I've been told, I wasn't an easy baby, either. I didn't sleep well, and I never wanted to be away from my mom. If she tried to leave me anywhere, I would cry until I made myself sick. Sounds like a challenge for even the most seasoned of mothers. But she loved me with all she had to give.

God blessed my mom with an amazing husband when I was five years old. I finally had a daddy. I had begged my mom to get me one for years, and there he was. What an awesome father, too. Even though he was only 21 at the time, he took me as his own daughter and poured his heart and soul into my life. Happy times followed as the three of us became a family. Three years later, my baby sister was born. She was conceived in love, and her birth was celebrated by us all. Especially me. I had prayed my heart out for her. Four years later, my brother was born, and our family was complete.

We had a lot of fun as a family. Things were good. But deep inside my unsuspecting heart were the unhealed wounds of a baby girl. Wounds that the Father wanted to get His hands on.

Not a Mistake

Near the end of another conference I attended, time was set aside for ministry. Soft music was playing, and prayers for healing began. It did not take long for people to begin weeping as their hearts were touched by pure love. I was sitting in my chair, repenting for the things that were coming to my mind and thanking God for the new understanding and truth I was receiving. I was totally unprepared for what came next.

"There are some of you here in this room tonight who may believe that your birth was a mistake." The man praying had barely finished saying the words when my body began to shake and tears began to stream from my eyes. I was caught off guard by my reaction to these words because I had never consciously thought of myself as a mistake. After all, I had been blessed with wonderful parents and a good life, and no one had ever told me I was a mistake.

Even so, I felt compelled to get out of my seat and move toward the front of the room. I joined all the others whose hearts were being laid open before the Lord, and found a small place on the floor. I got down on my hands and knees, almost in a fetal position, and listened as the prayers continued.

Somehow (I know it may sound crazy, but this is how the Holy Spirit works), I began to see where my orphan mentality had started. I caught a mental glimpse of myself awaiting the time of my birth, knowing that my life wasn't planned. I could sense that it wasn't a great time for me to be born, and I could see that there was no earthly father waiting to celebrate my life. I was also able to see that my infant heart was vulnerable at the time, and into it, Satan was whispering a lie: "You are a mistake, little girl. No one is happy that you are being born." For some reason, my little soul accepted that lie. Deep within, I believed that I was a mistake. No safe place, no inheritance, no celebration. God was showing me that I had been living with that well-hidden lie ever since.

It was time for that lie to be exposed and destroyed. The Father lovingly spoke to my heart and said, "Look at whose hands are waiting to bring you into life." Again, in my mind, I could see the delivery room. This time, it wasn't empty. This time, He was there. There might not have been an earthly father in the room, but my Heavenly Father was! His hands were outstretched, waiting to catch me as I was born. His face was lit up with excitement as He looked lovingly at my precious newborn body and into my little eyes.

"I'm excited that you are here," He said. "I've planned this day since before the beginning of time."

The truth that my life was not a mistake, combined with the tangible presence of the Father in that moment, had me undone. Tears poured down my face. With each tear came more healing and more experiential knowledge of the Father's love. I was overwhelmed with His goodness and gentleness. A major lie of the enemy had been exposed in my heart, and light was displacing the darkness. I was feeling freedom like I had never known.

It did not matter that I had not been conceived in love. It did not matter that my conception had not been planned by my earthly parents. It did not matter what my biological father felt for me. My true Daddy wanted me desperately. My Heavenly Father celebrated, and that's all that truly matters.

The Father's Thoughts

The enemy of our souls does not like for us to discover his lies. The truth we claim must be defended, and we can only defend the truth by knowing it. Many scriptures prove the heart of the Father toward us, and I cling to these scriptures whenever I sense that the Liar has come back to try to oppress me. Satan would love nothing more than for us to believe we are a mistake, that our Heavenly Father has no great plans for us. But these are lies. We must not believe him.

Whenever I am tempted to fall back into living like I'm an orphan or when I feel the enemy pressing in, I remind myself of the following truths from God's Word:

- The Father loves me so much that he knows everything about me. (Psalm 139:1–3)
- He pays so much attention to me that He knows the number of hairs on my head. (Matthew 10:29–31)
- The Father knew me even before I was conceived. (Jeremiah 1:4–5)
- I was not a mistake; He has plans for all my days. (Psalm 139:15–16)
- The Father wanted me to live. In fact, He knitted me together in my mother's womb. (Psalm 139:13)
- The Father brought me forth on the day I was born. (Psalm 71:6)
- He wants to spoil me with His love and blessings just because I'm his child. (1 John 3:1)
- The Father has great plans for my life. I don't have to be jealous of others. (Jeremiah 29:11)

- He is able to do more for me than I could possibly ask or think. (Ephesians 3:20)
- The Father loves me so much He wants to comfort me during every painful time of my life. (2 Corinthians 1:3–4)
- He thinks of me very much. In fact, His thoughts are more numerous than the sands by the sea. (Psalm 139:17–18)

A Healing Prayer

Oh Heavenly Father,

Thank You so much for Your amazing love for me. I can't believe how faithfully and completely You love me. I thank You that You have called me Your child and that You accept me no matter what state I am in.

I need to ask You to forgive me, Father, for all the years I have lived as if I were an orphan in Your house. Forgive me for having such a jealous and bitter heart, despising others for the blessings You've bestowed on them. Forgive me for all the years that my service in Your house was selfishly motivated. I know now that I was desperately trying to get my approval needs met in a place that You never intended them to be. Please forgive me for using my brothers and sisters in Christ for my own selfish gain, for looking to them to applaud me and promote me. I have been so wrong.

I now accept my place at Your table as Your daughter. I believe and confess that You have a plan and an inheritance for me. I do not need to be jealous of the gifts and callings You place upon others, for You have blessed me with unique gifts and Your plans for me are good. I choose to believe the truth of Your word about my life and the importance of it.

You are so good, Father, and I thank You for sending my Lord Jesus Christ to bring me back into Your arms of love. Thank you, Lord Jesus, for being the way, the truth, and the life. Thank You for paying the price for my sins of jealousy and selfishness. You are amazing.

I pray for the restoration of all that the enemy meant to steal from me. I claim my inheritance in the name of Jesus Christ, and I assume my position as a joint heir with Him.

In the most high name of Jesus,

Amen

CHAPTER FIVE

UGLY ROOTS

Pull dandelions until the sun goes down,
But unless you destroy the roots,
You will awaken to a garden of weeds.

I don't really know how it worked, but getting a deeper revelation of the Father's true heart for me gave me a new desire to live. It was such a relief to have burdens I had carried for years taken away: some burdens I had recognized and some I had not. I was no longer experiencing suicidal thoughts, and I was intent on living my life in a new way. I knew there was no need to be jealous anymore, and I believed God had a unique inheritance for me. I was experiencing freedom from much pain, but something ugly kept popping up here and there— something ugly and powerful.

One thing I have been blessed with is an amazing church family. The people are wonderful, and the leadership truly has a heart after God. My pastor and his wife, along with several other people, have loved me through many, many seasons of my life. They were there for me when my first marriage ended. They supported me when I was a single mother and patiently loved me through every stage of my Christian growth, including the years I lived as an orphan. They have always been an encouragement—in reality.

I say "in reality" because it is true. The problem is, once again, that I had a perception problem for many years, a problem that the Father so lovingly revealed to me as a continuation of the new things I was experiencing. More chains that I could not see were keeping me from truly being free, and He wanted them broken. Deep in my heart, so did I.

My need for further help started to become clear to me when, several Sundays in a row, I came home from church angry. It seemed I would go to church hopeful and expectant and leave feeling an emptiness that I couldn't describe. I found myself back on the bed in depression, and it troubled me greatly because I had been experiencing such growth in the Lord.

My husband would try to help me figure out the problem. One thing that was bothering me was the fact that I was bothered. I knew enough about the Lord to know that what I was feeling inside was not from Him. I was feeling resentment and anger, and quite honestly, I wanted to leave my church, a place that had been home to me for more than ten years.

An honest look back on each Sunday's events would reveal this: I had gone to church feeling that I deserved to have my special contribution to the body of Christ acknowledged, called out, and affirmed. When this hadn't happened in the way I had thought it should, I would leave feeling empty. If I hadn't been asked to be a part of the inner workings of a special event, I felt unneeded. When I saw others having what appeared to be deep and meaningful conversations, I felt left out. I would leave feeling deeply hurt even though no real wrong had been done. I was not being left out of anything, but in my deceived mind, I was being rejected.

The Tidal Wave

Someone once said that if you throw a small pebble into a pond, you should see only a small wave. Well, the small pebbles were beginning to cause tidal waves in my life.

My feelings of rejection came to a head one lovely afternoon at a baby shower being held for one of the young women in our church. There was great fellowship and food, and soon it was time for the expectant mother to open her gifts. Before she did, someone began to ask the pastor's and elders' wives one by one if they would come over to pray for the woman and the new baby. Being one of the elder's wives, I expected that my name would soon be called. One by one, I heard every name called but mine. The praying began. This was, in reality, a pebble. I know the woman who was calling for prayer. She is precious and loves me, and I honestly believe it was an oversight—now. At the time, though, I felt so rejected that I wanted to throw up.

It really did feel like a tidal wave inside me. My stomach was in a knot, and all I wanted to do was run out of the place. Because everyone was in the middle of praying, leaving would have been rude. I decided that I needed to think of the grossest thing I could to keep myself from totally losing it. So I thought of my dog sniffing a dead cow's rear end (something that had really happened that morning). Women all around me were rejoicing over a new life soon to enter the kingdom of God, and my mind was on—well, you know.

I was absolutely devastated. *How could they leave me out?* I thought. *Why don't they want me to pray with them? What's wrong with me?*

As soon as I possibly could, without looking too obvious, I left the place. I walked quickly to my car without looking back. It was a long walk, and all along the way, I was mentally shooting the bird at everyone I'd left behind. I made a mental decision that I did not need any of them anymore and didn't want to see them again.

I finally made it to my van and peeled out. The drive home was a tearful one. My heart was hurting desperately, and I couldn't believe what had just happened. Sunday after Sunday, I had left church feeling rejected, and now this. It seemed that the hits just kept coming, and finally, I had been knocked out of the fight.

As soon as I got home, I ran to my bedroom and slammed the door. The pain I was feeling was so intense that

I almost could not breathe. I cried out to the Father, "What is wrong with me? Why do I get hurt everywhere I go when I know in my mind there is truly nothing to feel hurt about? I can't take it anymore. Show me the root of this. I need to see it." It did not take long for Him to answer my request.

Stolen Innocence

As I lay on my bed crying for answers, the Holy Spirit once again came to show me some things. What He showed me was not fun to see, but it was so necessary.

Into my mind came a memory from my childhood. I was seven or eight years old, and I was visiting my aunt in Florida. Although I didn't really want to stay when my mom left, it seemed right for me to spend some time with my cousins. It was okay for a while, but then my aunt left for work. My cousins and I were then in care of her husband, my uncle.

Not long after my aunt left, my uncle told us that we were all going to play a game. I knew what was coming because I had played his "game" before. It was a version of hide and seek. He would hide our underwear, and we would have to search the house for them, naked. "If you can't find them," he would say, "then I get to do what I want to you."

"Please let us just have to brush our teeth," I begged him with fear filling every inch of my body.

"No," he laughed. "Now get going." Off we would go on a pointless yet desperate search for our panties. He would watch us and grin. The game was fixed from the start.

My mind was brought to what happened next, the point when my uncle got to do "what he wanted." My little hands were tied, my body pulled to the floor. My cousin was directed to get a washcloth to stuff into my mouth so my screams could not be heard by neighbors. My heart raced.

The tears ran down my cheeks as this big man molested my young body.

"Why did you let that happen to me, Lord?" I cried. "Wasn't I precious enough to protect?" I was thinking of my own children and how sweet they are, and the thought of them being treated this way made me absolutely sick. Then I thought of myself as a little girl. Wasn't I sweet enough to protect? Didn't my life have value?

Into my heart came the Father's gentle response: *"It was not My will for you to be hurt. It is never My will for My children to be abused. Though it is hard for you to understand, I was there protecting you. I was protecting your heart, the part of you that would later respond to my voice."*

The words did bring me some comfort, but it was the simple revelation that came next that had a profound impact on me. I could see in my mind how vulnerable my little heart had been at the time of this abuse. I could see how scared and insecure I had been, and I could also see that the Devil had been aware of it, too. Seeing how hurt I was, the enemy had seized the opportunity to speak lies into my young and vulnerable mind. "You are unimportant, little girl," he seethed. "Your life has no value. No one even wants to protect you. No one cares about you."

While recalling this time and crying out on my bed, I visualized the enemy whispering the words into my little ears. The sight of this made me mad because I knew that I had lived my life believing him. I had been living in pain, receiving rejection where there was absolutely no real reason for me to receive it simply because of a lie I had been told as a child. I thought about all the times I had been mad at my friends for leaving me out. I thought about the times I had left my precious church family feeling hurt and angry, and I could clearly see that they had not rejected me at all.

The Devil's lie had made absolutely innocent situations seem like painful arrows directed at my heart. Seeing this was the first step toward getting out of that trap. Healing for the wound was the next.

The Healing

Discovering Satan's lie made me want to rise up like a warrior and cut him through with a sword. That is exactly what the Father handed me next. Our sword in His kingdom is His Word, which is truth. As I lay there reeling from my new bird's-eye view of the enemy's tactic, the healing ointment of truth was poured over my broken heart.

God did not only want me to clearly see what the enemy had been doing at the time of my wounding; He also wanted me to see what He had been doing at that time, too. My mind was again directed back to the scene in my childhood, but this time I saw someone new in the room. I saw Him there. In the corner had been the Lord, Jesus, kneeling as if in prayer, tears streaming down His face as He had watched what was happening to me. I could see in His eyes that He was hurting more than I was. I could see that He had hated what He was observing more than I had hated experiencing it. I could see in the way He was rocking back and forth that I was desperately important to Him.

While I was seeing all of this in my mind, I heard the Father speak to my heart: *"You are so precious to me. I love you with an everlasting love. Your life has incredible value to Me, so much so that I sent My son to die to pay the price for the wrong that has been done to you. The tears you see Jesus crying are tears of pain. He was wounded, too, in so many ways. I hate it that you were abused. You are My little girl, in whom I am well-pleased. I want you. I choose you. You are mine."*

Again, I can't completely comprehend how the Holy Spirit works, but as these words filled my mind, I could actually feel change occurring in me. I could tangibly feel the arms of the Father scooping me up and cradling me in His arms as the tears continued to roll down my face. For so many years, I hadn't even been aware that I needed this moment. But it was then very clear that I needed to know that my life mattered. The wounds that were deeply hidden in my heart needed healing for me to truly be free from the sinful behaviors and thought patterns that were plaguing me.

It was incredibly liberating for me to learn that God really desired to address the wounds of my youth. For some reason, I had been under the impression that once you receive Jesus as your Savior, all things are new, and you shouldn't even look back. I had believed that all I needed to do was claim the truth of God's Word, and that would be good enough. Any time I was hurting or didn't feel like things were quite right inside me, I had figured I should just renew my mind and get my head out of my rear, or change my attitude. I knew that Jesus came to heal us, but I had figured that was a once-and-for-all kind of thing. We are healed at the altar, and that's that.

Well, we are truly healed once and for all, but that doesn't mean that God doesn't want to heal each and every wound of our souls in a personal way. God doesn't expect us to just get over the wounds of our life. He doesn't expect us to just act like things are okay. He wants to pour His transforming love into the very places of wounding so we can be truly healed and set free from the lies and bondage that we may have internalized as a result of being hurt. We can't rebuke our wounds. We can't just tell our wounds they don't exist or ignore them. We need to experience healing to truly be set free.

> *"'For I will restore health to you and heal you of your wounds,' says the Lord." (Jeremiah 30:17)*

"The Lord builds up Jerusalem; He gathers together the outcasts of Israel. He heals the broken-hearted, and binds up their wounds." (Psalms 147:2–3)

Are You Wounded, Too?

As human beings, we are created with basic needs. Our physical needs are things such as food, water, shelter, and clothing. It is also apparent that we have basic emotional needs. There are four basic human emotional needs agreed on by many counselors and pastors:

1. **Unconditional love**—love that is spoken to us and expressed in a physical way, such as hugs and kisses
2. **Security**—a feeling of security and physical and emotional safety (not just having roofs over our heads)
3. **Praise**—being affirmed, valued, and admired by another
4. **Purpose**—a reason to be alive and a hope for the future

Having all of these needs met makes for a perfectly healthy person. Any time these needs are neglected or threatened, however, wounds can occur in our souls. From what I've learned, it doesn't matter if the problem was direct physical or emotional abuse or an unintentional failure to meet any or all of the four basic needs. Either way, it can cause us to develop habits of thoughts or behaviors that keep us from experiencing all that the Word of God says we should.

When we are born again into the family of God, we receive His life into our spirits. This is where the Holy Spirit dwells. But we are not only spirit beings. We have two other areas of our being to deal with: the body and soul. I think we can all agree that once we leave the altar and say the sinner's prayer, life doesn't suddenly become perfect. This is because we have only been made perfect in our spirits. If the Holy Spirit dwells there, you can't get more perfect than that.

The area of the soul, or the heart, is commonly recognized as the area of mind, will, emotions, and personality. It is in this area that we may see the effects of emotional wounds in our lives. For me, the most obvious manifestations of wounding were the amount of jealousy I felt throughout my life and the rejection I internalized. There are many more actions or attitudes that might be manifestations of wounded hearts. I learned about these at a Shiloh Place Ministries school I attended on dealing with wounded hearts:

1. **Withdrawal or isolation**—cutting ourselves off from people, thinking they are unsafe or a source of pain
2. **Walls of self-protection**—fear of man with possible aggression
3. **Possessiveness**—bonding to only one or two people and becoming threatened by others trying to enter into those relationships
4. **Control and manipulation**—aggressive control or subtle manipulation to be in charge
5. **Difficulty receiving correction or instruction**—having a hard heart toward others and being very opinionated
6. **Difficulty in receiving or giving love and acceptance**—having a hard time expressing emotions
7. **Constant need of attention or recognition**—needing constant praise and steering conversations toward one's own achievements
8. **Feeling of being unloved and drawing rejection out of others**—feeling betrayed easily and being suspicious—setting oneself up for rejection but blaming others for it

9. **Self-centeredness**—having a victim mentality—always needing people to pray for oneself; showing little interest in others' needs
10. **Emotional immaturity**—not knowing how to have mature relationships
11. **Patterns of broken relationships**—distrusting, hindering the ability to bond in a healthy way
12. **Trouble finding identity in a group**—fighting to fit in because one have learned to follow and not lead; unhealthy need for acceptance
13. **Judgmental attitude**—building oneself up by putting others down
14. **Lack of intimacy with God**—blaming God for the bad things that have happened in one's life; transferring one's feelings toward authority to God
15. **Fears and phobias**—having a deep fear of man, rejection, failure, people's faces, intimacy, loving again, not being in control, panic attacks, etc., as a result of wounding
16. **Argumentativeness and quick-temperedness**—being impatient of others who don't think the same; using anger as a means of controlling others; having a deep need to be right because being wrong means one is broken, has no value, and isn't loved and accepted
17. **Lack of self-discipline and responsibility**—having low levels of responsibility at home, work, or church; no discipline with finances, or personal appearance
18. **Over-responsibility**—having a perfectionist mentality; having to have everything in its place to feel good

19. **Self-rejection, no self-worth**—living with much guilt and shame; wishing to end life; suppressing anger, resulting in depression

Reading the Bible teaches us that the above characteristics are not godly. But this knowledge alone will not take the behaviors and thoughts away. I know now that part of the reason for my severe depression was the fact that I had carried so many of these ungodly beliefs with me for so many years of my Christian life. The difference between what the Bible said I should be feeling and what I actually was experiencing was painfully confusing to me.

Position versus Experience

God's Word describes for us the many things we can experience once we choose to live our lives in His kingdom. We read that because of what Jesus did for us on the cross, we have been blessed with amazing identities. We see things like:

- I am a new creation (2 Corinthians 5:17)
- I am God's workmanship created in Christ (Ephesians 2:10)
- I am Christ's friend (John 15:15)
- I can do all things through Christ (Philippians 4:13)
- I am joined to the Lord and am one spirit with Him (1 Corinthians 6:17)
- I am an expression of the life of Christ (Colossians 3:4)

All of these statements are true. Because they are true, they are indeed our *position* in Christ. Our position in Christ is the perfect plan of God. The problem is that, a lot of times, our *experiences* do not match up to our positions. Many days I proclaimed to the air, "I am more than a conqueror," and then sat down, overwhelmed with feelings of defeat. I can't even recall the number of times I said, "I can do all things through Christ," and then failed yet another diet. There was a big disconnect between what the Word says is true of me and what I was feeling.

Early on in our Christian experiences, many of us experience some major changes in our lives. I almost immediately lost many of my worldly desires. Within the first year of being a Christian, I lost the desire to smoke or hang out in bars. No longer did I have a desire to talk like a sailor. Some major changes occurred in my behavior.

Over the years, God continued to change me in other ways. This is our sanctification process, the way in which God changes us more and more into His image and nature. But after a while, it seemed like my sanctification process slowed down. I became very frustrated by the areas in which my experience was not matching up to my position. At times I felt hopeless because the truth of God's Word didn't seem to be working for me. I didn't feel joy, or peace, and I definitely did not feel patient. I felt almost empty inside. This is part of why I wanted so desperately for God to take me or change me.

I can see now that one of the biggest hindrances to me experiencing what God says is true was the area of wounding in my soul. I had His spirit living in me, which is why I felt grieved about my experiences, but I needed healing to be set free. I needed to have His light shed on the dark areas of my heart where the enemy had me deceived. Once I realized that our Heavenly Father longs to heal us and that the enemy likes to lie to us in our weakest moments, I felt my sanctification process speed up again. It was like a snowball picking up momentum with each revolution!

Steps toward Healing

I don't think everyone's path toward healing is the same, but I do believe there are some basic keys toward setting off in the right direction. First of all, I believe that we won't ask for help unless we are aware that we need it. In most recovery circles, the first step toward getting help is admitting there is a problem. So, to begin with, we need to be aware that there could be areas in our hearts that are wounded. We may need to set aside some pride to admit this.

If we are experiencing enough pain as a result of the wounding in our lives, whether or not we realize it is from wounding, we will cry out for help. We then need to be willing to receive what the Father has to give, no matter how uncomfortable the process may be at times. The first thing He longs for us to receive is His unconditional love. As I said earlier, we must lose any misconceptions we have of His heart and His nature. We will not be able to receive love from a Father we don't know and trust. We've got to ask Him to reveal to us His true nature.

Next, we need to ask Him to reveal to us the truth about who we are. We need to believe that we are His children, created for a purpose with an inheritance of our own, and that He absolutely adores us. We have got to believe that He has good things in store and that we are very valuable to Him.

Then, we need to believe that He loves us so much that He wants to heal all of our wounds. He is not interested in children who behave outwardly as if all is well. He wants things to actually *be* well. It is okay to ask Him to show you the areas of your heart that are wounded. It is okay to look back at your life to see where the enemy may have introduced a lie into your heart that is causing you to live short of God's promises for you. It is important to understand that we are not looking back to blame anyone for our pain but to discover a cause-and-effect relationship. If we are not living out of our true position in Christ, we want to find out why and get it set straight.

Getting our wounds healed will put a stop to any cycles of wounding that may be taking their courses in our lives. I can clearly see a cycle that was at work in my past. The negative thoughts I had about my friends both in childhood and in adult years led to sin and disobedience in my life such as talking badly about others and coveting what they had. These actions led to a feeling of spiritual numbness where God's light could not shine—spiritual darkness—because our sin separates us from God. Spiritual darkness in my life led to my desire to die. I know who wants me dead—the Devil.

God longs to break this cycle in our lives, and He can if we will receive the healing. The path to healing also requires repentance and forgiveness. This was the next step for me.

Healing Prayer

Heavenly Father,

I love You and thank You for Your amazing love for me. I choose to receive Your love into my heart in greater amounts today. I choose to believe what Your Word says is true of me and nothing else. You are the source of my life.

Lord, there are areas of my heart where I don't seem to be experiencing all that Your Word says I could be. I seem to keep falling into a trap of ungodly thoughts and behaviors that I know are not pleasing to You. I am grieved by my inability to live the abundant life You've promised me. I need Your help.

Father, I hand over my heart to You, in its entirety. I lay down any pride that would keep me from true transparency before You. If my sinful patterns are a result of wounding in my life, I want to see it so I can be healed. I want to be as David was, a man of great transparency before You. Search me and see if there be any wicked way in me, Father. Search me and show me if there is wounding that needs to be healed.

I want to be healed, Father. I trust You to pour Your healing love over my heart. I believe that You want to reveal to me the truth in places where the enemy has lied to my soul. I want to see the truth, Father. I want to see it.

I no longer want to live my life believing the lies of Satan. His lies have kept me from experiencing true freedom for far too long. In the name of Jesus, I claim victory over my enemy. I choose to walk in the light of my Father God. I choose to live in Your truth.

Prepare my heart to forgive any who may have wounded me in my life, intentionally or not. Prepare my heart to take responsibility for my own sinful reactions to the wrongs done to me. I give You permission to change me through and through, Father. I want nothing less than your best for my life.

I love you, Lord, and I lift my eyes to you and you alone.

In the name of my precious Savior, Jesus Christ,

Amen

CHAPTER SIX

FESSING UP

All indifference to others' needs;
All indifference to others' feelings; all sharp and hasty judgments and utterances;
All manifestations of temper;
All touchiness and irritations;
All feelings of bitterness;
All feelings of separation and isolation;
Have their roots in pride!
Pride ever seeks itself!

-Andrew Murray "Humility"-

For many years, my heart was like a clogged well. When I accepted Jesus as my Savior, I received a deposit of living water. The living water brought new life, but it could not complete its ultimate purpose: to flow out of me onto others. The areas of darkness that had clogged my well were still there, keeping the water level from rising.

Thankfully, the heavenly plumber arrived to deal with the clog. The first thing He did was pour huge amounts of His love over me. As soon as I began to receive it, the blockages were loosened. First, he revealed to me my misconceptions of Him as my Father. Then, I saw how I had been living as if I were an orphan in His kingdom, as if no good thing would ever come to me. Next, He exposed areas of my heart that were desperately wounded and in need of healing—healing He was waiting to bring.

All of these encounters with God's truth brought greater and greater measures of peace and life. My depression was virtually gone. I began to experience joy like never before, true joy that is not circumstantial but positional. I was actually beginning to believe that God did have life for me that was more than abundant. I had never quite understood or believed this before.

As the blockages in my heart were being dealt with one by one, I began to feel the level of living water rise within me. For the first time, I felt true love for my friends. I felt myself being more interested in their lives and in their hearts. For so many years, my focus had been on myself. My wounded heart could not even begin to truly love another, no matter how I tried to fake it.

The life that was flowing through me was better than anything I had ever experienced before. Nothing feels as good as freedom. Galatians 5:1 had a deeper meaning to me: *"Stand fast therefore in the liberty by which Christ has made us free, and do not be entangled again with a yoke of bondage."*

Jesus set us free on Calvary not only to provide us with eternal life but also to provide us with freedom during this life. Seeing this made me want more. If Jesus died so I can be free, then I wanted all I could get. "Bring it on, Lord," I prayed. "Give me all that You've got." Of course, He answered my prayer.

Can You Forgive?

My relationship with the Father was definitely better than it had ever been. Because I don't live on a deserted island with only Him, there were other relationships I needed to get straight. The next step in my healing process was forgiving those who had hurt me.

God's heart is very clear on this issue:

> *But I say to you who hear; Love your enemies, do good to those who hate you, bless those who curse*

> *you, and pray for those who spitefully use you. To him who strikes you on one cheek, offer the other also. And from him who takes away your cloak, do not withhold your tunic either. Give to everyone who asks of you. And from him who takes away your goods do not ask them back. And just as you want men to do to you, you also do to them likewise. But if you love those who love you, what credit is that to you? For even sinners love those who love them. And if you do good to those who do good to you, what credit is that to you? For even sinners do the same. And if you lend to those from whom you hope to receive back, what credit is that to you? For even sinners lend to sinners to receive as much back. But love your enemies, do good, and lend, hoping for nothing in return; and your reward will be great, and you will be sons of the Highest. For He is kind to the unthankful and evil. Therefore be merciful, just as your Father is merciful. (Luke 6:27–36)*

I always knew that God was a god of forgiveness. I knew that we are supposed to forgive one another, and there were many things along the way that I could forgive. If a friend didn't call when she said she would, I could forgive that. If my husband came home later than he had anticipated from work, I could forgive that. But being able to truly forgive the man who had stolen my innocence as a young girl, who had defiled my little body and broken down my boundaries, making me a target for every predator around—that would be more difficult. I did not know how to do it. No matter how much I thought I had let it go, the memory of that man would bring murderous thoughts into my head. I wanted him to pay for what he had done to me. I felt he deserved to be hanged—by his genitals.

Then the Holy Spirit began His work on me again. Somehow, I became willing to become willing to forgive the man. I acknowledged the fact that it was necessary, and I believed that if the Father was asking it of me, it was for my good. His amazing love surrounded me and filled me with each step I took in the direction of forgiveness. It was not a journey I was expected to take alone.

I began to understand that for a man to defile a child the way my uncle had, there must be some deep wounding in his heart. People who are loved and are well do not hurt others. I don't know for sure how my uncle grew up, but I do know that he was not getting his love needs met from Father God. Somehow along the way, he had believed a lie, a lie that he could get his needs met by molesting children. It is a perversion of God's intended plan, but that's what the Devil does best: pervert God's plans.

I could just imagine what kind of a childhood my uncle must have had. Maybe he was berated by his father. Maybe he himself had been molested as a young boy, and at his most vulnerable and frightened moment, the Devil had made his move. Somewhere along the way, a young boy had been wounded, and the unhealed wound had festered and led him into a life of sin and perversion.

Seeing my perpetrator through the eyes of Jesus gave me the ability to take the next step. Being a wounded man did not excuse his actions. It was not okay for him to take out his pain on me. But, because of God's Spirit living in me, I began to feel mercy for him—mercy that enabled me to take him off the gallows in my mind and hand him over to God.

Forgiveness does not mean that we have to be in relationships with those who have hurt us. It doesn't mean we have to trust them, either. If you bump me every time you walk by, I can forgive you for that, but next time you walk by, I will move. Forgiveness simply means being willing to take those who have injured us off our "hook" and put them on God's. We must trust that God will deal justly with them, and we must be okay with the outcome that God chooses.

Forgiveness is a process. It does not come over night, and sometimes is scary and painful. Letting go of control, even though it is imagined, is not easy. I could sense, however, that as I allowed myself to see things God's way, bit by bit, the forgiveness came. With each step I took, I realized that the forgiveness I was giving was not for my uncle but for me. By forgiving my uncle, I was, in fact, opening the door to further healing in my own heart. I was being set free. Unforgiveness is a heavy burden, one I had been carrying for many years. It had blocked the flow of God's love in my life, and by relinquishing it, I was receiving the blessings.

> *"Finally, all of you be of one mind, having compassion for one another; love as brothers, be tenderhearted, be courteous; not returning evil for evil or reviling for reviling, but on the contrary blessing, knowing that you were called to this, that you may inherit a blessing." (1 Peter 3:8–9)*

What about the Others?

My uncle wasn't the only person I needed to forgive. For many years, I was not consciously aware of it, but I was harboring unforgiveness toward my parents. When the process of healing started in my life and I was reminded of the painful events in my childhood, deeply hidden resentments began to surface.

Even though my parents did not know what my uncle had been doing to me in secret (and you can imagine what they wanted to do when they did find out), in my little-girl heart, them leaving me with him felt like a betrayal. I wanted them to somehow know what was happening and protect me from it. Deep within my heart was unforgiveness toward my parents even though they hadn't purposely done anything to hurt me.

Seeing that I held unforgiveness in my heart toward my parents was painful. They were great parents. They made many sacrifices for me over the years and poured their hearts and souls into me. Because they were so wonderful to me, I felt guilty that I needed to forgive them. It felt like I was betraying them, but denying what I really felt inside would have left seeds of bitterness in my heart, seeds that I knew would not lie dormant.

Once again, with my hand in Father God's hand, I walked to the foot of the cross. There, I gently placed my mom and dad at the feet of Jesus and made a decision to forgive them. In my heart I knew they had always loved me to the best of their ability. I knew that they did not intentionally allow harm to come my way, and I knew that if they could go back in time to change it, they would.

Placing my wound and those I needed to forgive at the foot of the cross made the way for even more healing to come into my heart. No longer was my identity going to be tied to that wound. I could finally walk away from it and turn my whole attention to the Father. It is from Him and Him alone that we must get our identities.

"And you, being dead in your trespasses and the uncircumcision of your flesh, He has made alive together with Him, having forgiven you all trespasses, having wiped out the handwriting of requirements that was against us, which was contrary to us. And He has taken it out of the way, having nailed it to the cross." (Colossians 2:13–14)

Broken Laws

When He created the earth, God set into action certain physical laws such as the laws of gravity, inertia, and centrifugal force. Along the way on my journey, I learned that He also put into place certain spiritual laws. For example, in the beginning, God said, "*Therefore a man shall leave his father and his mother and be joined to his wife, and they shall become one flesh" (Genesis 2:24).*

The law God created here is that when a man and a woman cleave together and consummate their relationship with sexual intercourse, they shall become one flesh. This does not mean they literally become one body but that they become tied in a very intimate way. A soul tie is created between the man and woman who have committed to stay with each other for life.

It's a great spiritual law. The problem comes when people don't understand how it works. You see, even when a man and a woman who are not committed to each other for life have sexual relations, the same soul-tie happens. They become one flesh. When the relationship ends, it is devastating. In effect, a part of each has been deposited in the other and is taken away as they depart. I believe this law to be true, because I experienced the painful effect it had during my promiscuous years. With each person who used me and left, I felt a small piece of myself die. Now I understand why.

There are other spiritual laws God has put into place. A very important one is the law of honoring your parents:

"*Children obey your parents in the Lord, for this is right. 'Honor your father and mother,' which is the first commandment with promise: that it may be well with you and you may live long on the earth." (Ephesians 6:1–3)*

This law says that when we honor our parents, blessings will flow into our lives. It seems logical to say that if we don't honor our parents, the opposite will be true. We will actually suffer the consequences of breaking the law: loss of blessings.

Even though I was enjoying the lightheartedness and freedom that came as a result of my choice to forgive others, it did not take long for God to shine His holy flashlight into my heart again. Another area of darkness in my heart needed to be revealed.

A look back on my life brought to the front of my mind a clear vision of almost every time as a little girl that I had stuck out my tongue at my parents behind their backs. I remembered all the times I had destroyed their trust as a young teenager and flipped them off while driving away from their disappointed hearts. Then I saw the times I had actually cussed in my mother's face as a rebellious and deceived young woman. My spirit was grieved beyond words. I had lived my life as a law breaker, dishonoring my parents at every turn of my life.

There was yet another crime to add to my rap sheet: breaking the law of judging. The Bible says, *"Judge not, that you be not judged. For with what judgment you judge, you will be judged; and with the same measure you use, it will be measured back to you" (Matthew 7:1–2).* The Bible also says, *"Judge not, and you shall not be judged. Condemn not, and you shall not be condemned. Forgive, and you will be forgiven. Give, and it will be given to you, good measure pressed down, shaken together, and running over will be put into your bosom. For with the same measure that you use, it will be measured back to you" (Luke 6:37–38).*

I cannot even recall the number of times I said to myself, "I will never do it that way with my kids" or "I could never treat anyone that way" or "If I were in charge, everything would be different." I didn't know it at the time, but my condemning words, fueled by unrighteous anger and bitterness, were judgments that I was casting left and right. I had cast judgments on my parents. I had cast judgments on my employers. I had cast judgments on my church family, even my pastor.

Something I once read says this about the state we are in when we cast judgments: "Law demands that when we judge another judgment must come back on us (for every action, there is an equal and opposite reaction). It is not God's judging us, but the law."

I realized that I was undeniably a law breaker. The heaviness and godly sorrow I felt were immense, and I knew that what I needed to bring to the foot of the cross this time was my own sinful self.

Showered in the Blood

The only hope for a law breaker like me was to run to my Savior, Jesus Christ. At the cross, I knew, I would find forgiveness and mercy.

"Christ has redeemed us from the curse of the law, having become a curse for us." (Galatians 3:13)

Even as I began to acknowledge my own need for forgiveness for dishonoring the people I love, God continued to shine His loving, gentle light on other areas of sin in my heart. In Roy Hession's book, *The Calvary Road,* he sums up what I was seeing with this statement: "Anything that springs from self, however small it may be is sin. Self-energy or self-complacency in service is sin. Self-pity in trials or difficulties, self-seeking in business or Christian work, self-indulgence in one's spare time, sensitiveness, touchiness, resentment and self-defense when we are hurt or injured by others, self-consciousness, reserve, worry, fear, all spring from self and all are sin and make our cups unclean."

I didn't realize that there was so much sin in my heart. After all, I didn't smoke or party anymore. I wasn't cussing or stealing or abusing anyone. Oh, I was so blind.

Praise God that He loves us enough to show us all that stops us from receiving His life. Our sin represents spiritual darkness, and He is light. Where there is sin, there is no God. God is so good that I decided I wanted all of Him there is to have. I want to get rid of the darkness in my heart, whatever it takes. Fortunately, it takes only a two-step process:

"If we confess our sins, He is faithful and just to forgive us our sins and to cleanse us from all unrighteousness." (1 John 1:9)

Step one: confess our sins

Step two: He is faithful to forgive

Of course our confessions must be made with repentant hearts that desire to not only confess the sin but also make it right. We come to our loving Heavenly Father, let Him know we see our sins and are grieved by them and willing turn away and make it right, and He faithfully washes us clean.

I don't know about you, but I can do a two-step process. Understanding the freedom that comes from confession alleviates any aversion I used to have to the word "sin." Now, I'm on the lookout for sin in my heart. Show me my sin, Lord. Show me.

I finally understand why David was deemed a man after God's heart. Looking at this King's life, it would seem he was not a man for God. He did some pretty bad things. But a closer look shows what really matters: a man of true repentance.

> ***(To the Chief Musician. A Psalm of David, when Nathan the prophet came to him, after he had gone in to Bathsheba):*** *"Have mercy on me, O God, according to Your loving-kindness; according to the multitude of Your tender mercies, blot out my transgressions. Wash me thoroughly from my iniquity, and cleanse me from my sin. For I acknowledge my transgressions; and my sin is ever before me. Against You, You only, have I sinned, and done evil in Your sight; that You may be found just when You speak, and blameless when You judge. Behold, I was brought*

> *forth in iniquity, and in sin did my mother conceive me. Behold, You desire truth in the inward parts; and in the hidden part You shall make me to know wisdom." (Psalm 51:1–6)*

David was a man who was willing to have his sin revealed. He understood that confessing his sin would bring him life and wisdom. He lived ever asking the Father to search his heart: "*Create in me a clean heart, O God, and renew a steadfast spirit within me" (Psalm 51:10).*

I want to recognize my sin and have it washed clean, not because I think it will make God love me more but because He loves me so much. If there was a man on earth who loved me the way He does, I would do anything it takes to get closer to him. How much more should I want to do everything it takes to get closer to a God who is so desperately in love with me?

Ugly Pride

The Bible says that it is God's love and goodness that draws men to repentance (*Romans 2:4*). I believe that verse like never before, for the more I began to receive the love of the Father into my heart, the more I wanted to be rid of anything that was not of Him. I know it will be a lifelong search, and I am thankful that God has been kind enough to slowly reveal to me my sin. I know the weight of it would be too hard to bear all at once.

The more I began to accept (not just in my head but in my heart) the depths of the love being poured upon me, my spirit became increasingly grieved with the levels of pride I had been walking in. For many years, I had been easily offended. I had walked around blaming others for my problems, thinking that if others would change, my life would be better. If only others would notice me, or if only other people weren't such jerks, then things would be better. The chip on my shoulder wasn't always obvious to others because I wouldn't take it out until I was at home. Those closest to me had to bear the brunt of it.

Proverbs 16:18 says, "*Pride goes before destruction and a haughty spirit before a fall.*" I used to think that verse was talking about some sort of punishment for people who were conceited or arrogant. In my mind it applied to "them." I would think, *I'm so glad I'm not like* them. *They are really in for a fall.* But I finally realized that verse was a warning to me.

This warning is not that if I don't straighten up, God is going to punish me. What I believe this verse says is that pride makes a way for the enemy to do his stuff. Pride is the absence of humility. The Bible says that God resists the proud (*James 4:6*). Resisting implies staying away from something. If I'm filled with pride, then God is resisting that part of me. If God is staying away from a part of me, the enemy will make his move. He is sitting back, just waiting for areas of darkness to pop up in my life because that is his domain.

Jesus was not prideful. He did not think more highly of Himself than he ought. He did not carry offenses when others betrayed him. We don't ever see Him standing in a crowd saying, "Don't you realize who I am, people?" He had no chip on his shoulder. It was because of his total humility that he walked in such power. He did not do miracles in his own strength, but by the Father's. Because there was no pride in Jesus, there was nothing for the Father to resist; God was totally with Jesus at all times. Jesus walked in perfect harmony with His Father, and because of that, His life was filled with power.

If anyone had a right to feel bitter and resentful, it was Jesus. The very people He had come to save persecuted him and had him put to death. The most religious people of his time didn't even recognize that He was the son of God. He didn't care. As a matter of fact, most of the time, He didn't want anyone to recognize Him or the miracles He performed. He wanted all the glory to go to His father, for he understood this to be His sole purpose on earth: walking in perfect relationship with the Father that the world through him (Jesus) might be reconciled to Him (Romans 5:10).

Jesus was a wounded man, but He did not let his wounds cause Him to sin. Through His example, I can see that I am not responsible for the wounds inflicted upon me. It is not my fault if I am abused or hurt. But my reaction to the wounds is my responsibility. Even if my bitterness stems from a hurt, it is still bitterness. Jesus paid the price for that wound. In reality, I have no right to hold on to it. Furthermore, God is longing to heal it. For me to hang on to any ungodly beliefs or thought patterns is sin. The Father wants us to surrender any rights we think we have to hold on to our pain. He wants us to get out of victim mentality so we can be truly free.

God wants us to allow our pride and stubbornness to be broken because they are major tools the enemy uses to keep our hearts seething with anger and pain. If we let God break us, that is to bring about true humility before Him, living water begins to flow through us like never before.

In *The Calvary Road*, Roy Hession so beautifully says this: "In order to break our wills to His, God brings us to the Cross and there shows us what real brokenness is. We see those wounded hands and feet, that face of love crowned with thorns, and we see the complete brokenness of the One who said, 'Not my will, but Thine be done,' as He drank the bitter cup of our sin to its dregs. So the way to be broken is to look on Him and realize it was our sin which nailed Him there. Then as we see the love and brokenness of the God who died in our place, our hearts will become strangely melted, and we will want to be broken for Him."

Restitution

I did not sin all those years in isolation. The people in my life were affected by my bitterness and judgments, as well. With my need for repentance before the Father also came my need to make things right with the people whom I had wronged all these years. It was now time for me to ask for forgiveness from them.

The Bible says confessing our sins to one another brings us healing (James 5:16). I believe it brings healing because we have to lay down our pride to confess our gross stuff to someone else. Confession of my sins means that I need to be more concerned with what God thinks than what people think, and that is hard, especially when you have lived your life desperately needing the approval of man.

When we lay down our pride, God gives us grace, which is His power (James 4:6). We can then find the courage to go before man and repent for the wrongs we have done to them.

I knew in my heart there were some key people I needed to ask forgiveness of. First and foremost were my parents. I have now asked them on several different occasions to forgive me for things that have come to mind. I've asked my mom to forgive me for the judgments I had cast upon her in my heart and for the total lack of honor I had shown her in my youth. I've asked my dad to forgive me for dishonoring him, as well.

As I humbled myself before them, I could feel the Father smile. I believe He was smiling not because I was finally *doing* the right thing, but because He knew my willingness to lay down pride was kicking the Devil in the tail. Our Heavenly Father loves to see the father of lies exposed. He has been in the business of setting his children free since the very beginning.

One day at church I knew what I needed to do next. When the thought came to my mind, my heart began to race, and my face got hot. I knew I needed to ask my pastor and his wife to forgive me for the times I had been attending the church physically but not truly in my heart. I was confident that they would be merciful and would immediately forgive me, but I was ashamed of the fact that I had experienced seasons of such ugliness in my heart. I knew that I had to get over my humiliation and embrace *humility*. I knew I had to walk in obedience.

So at the end of service that day, before they could leave for lunch, I stopped my pastor and his wife and said something like this: "I need to ask your forgiveness. Will you please forgive me for not completely being underneath your ministries for so many years? Will you please forgive me for having a bitter spirit at times and not always believing the best in my heart? I understand that I have been living like an orphan, having an unhealthy need for your approval. That has not been fair to you. Will you please forgive me?"

They both looked at me with total love and full-heartedly gave me their forgiveness. The conversation did not take long, but I knew that it had eternal ramifications. I also knew that I had made myself even more accountable to maintaining the right heart from that moment forward. I had made a verbal statement to them and to the Lord saying that I knew I had been wrong and I would need to continue to live right to maintain the healing and freedom that would come.

There were some people I had condemned in my mind that I knew I should not actually confess to. Sometimes, confession of our sins might cause the other person to feel pain. I wouldn't want to say to someone, "Will you forgive me? I've always thought you were a real jerk; in fact, I've hated you." Obviously, this would not bring reconciliation between the two parties. It is very important to let the Holy

Spirit bring to mind who He wants us to confess our sins to. Sometimes it may be a trusted friend who isn't involved, someone who can pray with you and help keep you accountable.

Be aware that the enemy doesn't like to give up easily. With each step I've taken toward humility and restoration, he has tried to tempt me to fall back into bitterness and resentment and back into orphan thinking. People still have conversations without me at church. Events are still planned without my involvement. But now when the Devil tries to sneak in and say, "See, you aren't important; nobody cares about you," I just rise up and say, "Speak to the hand, the hand of my Heavenly Father, who adores me and has plans for my life."

The more I stand firm in the truth and the healing that has been given to me, the better I get at recognizing the Devil's schemes and resisting him. I like to watch him flee.

Healing Prayer

Precious Lord Jesus,

Thank You for dying on the cross so that the world would be saved through You. Thank You for your amazing humility, Your willingness to be broken in every way for me. Words are too feeble to express the praise and honor You deserve.

Holy Spirit, thank You for Your amazing love and wisdom. Thank You for so gently showing me the areas of my heart that have been filled with darkness. Thank You for lovingly showing me the areas of sin that have kept me from walking in the total healing and life I have been promised. Please continue to search my heart and reveal any blind spots I may continue to have.

Heavenly Father, thank You for forgiving me for my bitterness and the judgments I have made upon Your other children. Thank You for providing me with a safe place in Your arms to confess the areas of sin I see in myself. You are such a loving daddy. Thank You for not shaming me and condemning me for all the areas in which I have fallen short of Your glory.

I thank You for my parents, my husband and children, my friends, and my pastor and his family. I pray for amazing blessings to come to them all. I pray that You will restore to them any damages they may have accrued as a result of my resentment and pride. Bless them with Your amazing love. Please fill me with even more of Your love so that it can overflow out of me onto them like never before.

I choose to walk in humility before You and man. I give You permission to daily search my heart and see if there be any wicked way in me. I do not want to live in pride, Father, for I know that it is a dwelling place for my enemy. I do not want to live my life with the mentality of a victim, for You truly have paid the price for all wrongs done against me. Help me to continue to walk in that truth.

I love you, Father God. You are amazing, steady and unchanging. I embrace Your will for me. I embrace You. I embrace life.

In the healing name of Jesus,
Amen

PART THREE

WALKING IN VICTORY:
Loving My Big Butt

CHAPTER SEVEN

ENCOUNTER AT THE BEACH

And they were both naked,
The man and his wife;
And they were not ashamed.
-Genesis 2:25-

I was packing my suitcase and looking forward with great anticipation to the upcoming week. Bill and I had our children taken care of, and we were headed to Myrtle Beach, South Carolina, to attend a week-long ministry school on healing for wounded hearts. The great revelations and freedom that were transforming my life left me hungering to learn more so I could more effectively bring help to others.

I searched my closet for clothes that still fit me and weren't terribly worn out and folded them into my bags. I packed my toiletries and all the books I wanted to bring, as well as several taped teachings my husband and I hoped to listen to on our long drive. Before I zipped up my suitcase for good, there was one final decision I needed to make—one I had purposely left until the last minute: Would I pack my humiliation suit or not? Even as I made the decision to go ahead and pack it, my stomach knotted up. I hated that suit. It was my bathing suit.

Despite all the healing and new life that I had been experiencing since my journey to wholeness had begun, there was still a major issue that hadn't been solved in my life. I still hadn't found the root of why I couldn't get thin and why I kept failing at every diet I attempted. I was determined to get some major prayer for deliverance while at the ministry school. I was desperately hoping that whatever was keeping me overweight would be discovered so I could finally get the fat off my rear. I was also aching to rid myself of the ever-lingering sense of failure I carried.

My husband listened to me talk about my weight issues for hours on our trip to the coast. I tossed several ideas around that I felt might be the root of my weight issues. Maybe there was a very deeply seated wound related to the sexual abuse in my past. Maybe there was a generational sin passed down that needed to be renounced. Maybe there was a spirit of failure that needed to be rebuked. I didn't really know, but I knew I needed answers, because if I didn't get them, I might stay fat forever, and then I would never be truly beautiful.

I had experienced enough of God's light to feel that there was still a major area of darkness deep within me that needed to be dealt with. I just hadn't been able to see it yet. God had revealed many things to me, and I was on the search to find it all, so I had faith that I would soon find the final key to my deepest dreams, my dreams of being a thin woman and finally showing the world how gorgeous I was. I did find a key, but it wasn't to the door I was expecting.

Pray for Me Again, Please

Our week of training was off to a good start. The teachings confirmed much of what the Lord had been doing in my heart and deepened my desire to see others set free. It was a joy to engage in fellowship with people from different parts of the world, all seeking to understand the Father's heart in a deeper way. I was blessed, but I was still waiting to get my most important agenda underway: finding out what was still wrong with me.

After each session of teachings, the class broke out into small groups. The men and women were in separate groups, so that meant Bill and I had to split up. My group was small, about six women, and we started out by trying to get to know each other better.

The stage was set in hopes of open and honest communication. The leaders of the small group opened our time with prayer and then simply waited on someone to get the ball rolling. Because that person is almost always me, I made a conscious decision to keep my mouth closed. I knew it wouldn't be nice for me to monopolize the time or dominate the conversation, so I sat there quietly for as long as I could.

Finally, when the silence felt like impending doom, I had to speak. I didn't waste time with any trivialities. I needed to get my answers this week, and I was ready to get started. I don't recall exactly what I said, but I remember it was straight to the point. "I keep failing at diets, and I feel like there's something desperately wrong with me; something so hidden that I can't see it, and I need help."

The group leaders started asking me some basic questions, most likely in hopes that the answer would be something obvious. The other ladies in the group listened to my problems politely and even offered their ideas here and there. Finally, one of the leaders decided to pray for me.

I felt like I was holding my breath. I wanted so badly to have a supernatural enlightenment right then and there. I wanted to leave that little room a changed woman. I wanted to leave there so healed that I would have no appetite anymore and I would begin to see weight melt off of me. That's what I wanted. That's not what I got.

Another day of great teachings passed, and just as we had done the day before, the men and women divided into small groups. This time I was determined to keep my mouth shut. I didn't want to be seen as one of those people who always need to talk about themselves. So I bit my lip even though I secretly wished we could spend the entire time working on my issue.

Finally, a couple of other ladies shared a bit, and the room got quiet again. After a long stretch of silence, I offered to go see if the men were finished. They were still deep in discussion. If my small group were to dismiss, we would have to walk through the men's group to get out. Because we didn't want to disturb them, we were basically forced to extend our time together. Maybe I would get another shot after all.

I couldn't stay quiet any longer. I seized this unexpected opportunity to start another discussion on my issues. More questions were asked in hopes of getting to the root of my weight problem, and then the leaders decided to pray for me again. The prayers were wonderful and sweet, but when I left the school that day, I still had not found the answer to my questions. I didn't feel any different, and I wondered how I was every going to get fixed.

Return of My Worst Enemy

Back at the hotel room that night after classes, my husband suggested that we relax by going down to the hot tub. We only had a few more nights away together, and we were staying in a hotel that had a wonderful heated pool area. This was a great idea as far as he was concerned because in many ways, he is still like a little boy: he loves to play in water and he has no inhibitions about his body. He doesn't have any reason to feel self-conscious about his physical appearance anyway, because his body fits into the world's category of "looking good."

My body, on the other hand, did not look good. There wasn't a single part of me that had any desire to go down to that hot tub. All I wanted to do was put on my loose-fitting pajama pants and a big t-shirt and crawl under the covers. The sweet puppy-dog look I was getting from my husband really put me under pressure. I knew that I should go with him. I am his best friend. What fun would it be for him to go to a hot tub alone or splash around in a heated pool without company? What kind of a wife would I be if I didn't go with him? Still, I was kind of tired, so I asked him if it would be okay for me to pass, and being the understanding man that he is, he went down to the pool without me.

Bill loved the pool so much that the next night, he invited me to go with him again. This time I knew I had to go. It would be incredibly selfish for me to deny him this simple pleasure two times, even though it felt like a torture technique to me. So I excavated my bathing suit from the recesses of my bag and trudged slowly into the bathroom.

The wall-to-wall mirror that stood before me seemed to mock me even before my first piece of my clothing was shed. I tried not to look at my reflection while I undressed, but inevitably, I caught an unwanted glance at my naked body just as I went to grab my humiliation suit.

What I saw made me feel absolutely sick to my stomach. "Look at that fat on your stomach! How gross! Look at how big your rear is. Disgusting! You are so ugly. You will be a total embarrassment to your husband at the pool. You make me sick." My enemy in the mirror had returned to berate me with a vengeance.

With what little strength I had left, I wiggled into my bathing suit, attempting to ignore my enemy's evil glare. Once the suit was in place, I stole another glance at my reflection. Not much better. The fat on my stomach was covered up, but I could still see that it wasn't flat. My rear was covered, but there was no hiding the fact that it was big. And my pudgy arms only added to the disgraceful presentation. I began to cry. I hated being me, and puppy-dog eyes or not, I could not force myself to join my husband.

I quickly took off my swimsuit and escaped into the comfort of my large pajamas. When most of me was adequately covered, I emerged from the hell hole. "Bill, I'm sorry," I said, "but I can't go with you. I am so ugly and fat. I just can't be seen in my bathing suit." He went without me, again.

Once the door closed behind him, I fell on the bed in tears. I felt as if I were in a prison and as though there was never going to be a way out. I wanted so badly to understand what it was deep in me that kept me fat, what kept me unsuccessful at diets and thus feeling like the world's biggest failure. All the things God had been doing in my life were wonderful, but this one source of pain had incredible power over me. I knew I was missing out on much in life. I knew my family was not getting the best of me. I knew I could not live like this another day. I decided to go sit on the balcony, look out over the ocean, and have a good cry with my Daddy.

The Damascus Balcony

I opened the sliding-glass door that led to the balcony and was greeted with a gentle breeze rolling in off of the ocean. I sat down, pulled up a table to rest my feet on, and folded my arms across my chest. "Daddy, here I am," I said aloud. The fact that a guest in the adjacent room might be able to hear me didn't matter. I needed answers, and I wanted to make sure God could hear me loud and clear.

Without waiting for His reply, I set in with all my "why" questions. "Why am I so fat? Why can't I lose weight? Why is it so easy for everyone else in the world to lose weight, but I cannot seem to stay on a diet for more than a couple of weeks without blowing it? Why aren't you healing me of this? Why am I not getting answers this week when I drove almost ten hours, and I've been desperately searching my heart for the roots? Why, why, why…"

When I ran out of questions to ask, I just sat there crying. I didn't hear God answering me; I was aching for an audible response from Him. My heart felt like it was breaking inside of me. I felt as if I were drowning in the very ocean I was looking out upon. "Please, help me, Daddy. I need you so badly right now," I cried. "Please, please talk to me." Still no answer at first, but then, amazingly, He began to speak. When he did, the Father had a "why" question of His own.

"Teasi, Teasi, why are you calling me a liar?" I heard His voice gently say.

"What?" I replied, confused. This was not the answer I had expected to get. As a matter of fact, this was not an answer at all.

Then it came again, "Teasi, Teasi, why are you calling me a liar?" I sat very still, contemplating what I had heard. The feeling I had inside told me that this was definitely the Father. I was feeling a little nervous and excited, and I knew these were not mere thoughts of my own.

"What do you mean? I'm not calling you a liar. I love you. I'm here to learn how to share the truth of Your love to others, remember?" I was very confused and did not expect what came to me next.

This is what the Father had to say: "When you look into the mirror, you have a choice. You can choose whose opinion you are going to accept as truth. There are only two options: My opinion of you, and My enemy, Satan's, opinion. Whichever opinion you choose to accept, that is the one you believe to be true. All of your life, since you were a young girl, you have believed My enemy. You have been living your life as if what he says about you is the truth. This makes My opinion the one you choose not to accept; thus, you have been calling Me a liar."

The power of this revelation cut through me like a smoldering sword. Could it be true? Could I be calling the very God who had done so much to save me and heal me a liar? The possibility of this took my breath away. But there was more.

"Since your childhood, every time you have looked upon your reflection with disgust, you have linked arms with My enemy. Every time you said you were fat, every time you said you were ugly, every time you said you were a failure, you believed him over Me. My sweet daughter, if you think My opinion of you is a lie, then everything else I say must be a lie, too. When I say I created the earth, that must be a lie. When I say I saved Noah from the flood, that must be a lie. When I say I blessed Abraham to be a blessing to the nations, that must be a lie. When I say I sent My precious Son to die on the cross to pay the penalty for your sin, that must be a lie, too. In fact, everything in the book must be a lie, because if you think I'm lying about one thing, it makes Me a liar. Do you see?"

Just as with Saul on the road to Damascus, a heavenly light was shining all around me in my heart. In one instant, an instant when the Father decided to ask me a question for a change, my whole world seemed to stop. The truth of what I had been doing all of these years hit me like a semi truck, just as I'm sure it hit my brother, Saul. Then, trembling and astonished just as Saul was, I asked, "Daddy, what would you have me do?"

He lovingly replied, "Arise, go look into the mirror, and you shall be told what you shall do." With my eyes unblinded for the first time, I rose to face my enemy.

Enemies No More

When I walked into the bathroom, at first I couldn't look myself in the eyes. I felt so ashamed and full of sorrow that all of my life I had been linking arms with the Devil, the enemy of the God I loved so deeply. But I knew I needed to face this enemy of mine, the enemy who had followed me everywhere throughout my entire life. I looked up into the mirror and squarely into the reflection of my own eyes.

It was uncomfortable at first, looking at myself that way. In the past, I had never really wanted to look myself in the eyes because I had known I would see self-hatred. When you look deep into someone's eyes, it's almost as if you get a glimpse of his or her soul. For many years, I didn't want to face what I would have seen. Now I was facing it.

There was still self-hatred there. It was not fun looking at myself, but I stayed put, waiting for what would come next. Finally, I began to hear the voice of the Father again, gently pouring out His heart to me. What I heard went something like this: "Look into those beautiful blue eyes you've hidden from for so long. They are beautiful to Me, and I gave them to you so you could behold my wonders. Look at that beautiful face that shines with the reflection of My love when you let it. Look at those arms you think are so big and unattractive. They are precious to Me, and I gave those to you so you could hold My babies and hug My hurting children. Look at that stomach that disgusts you so. I love that stomach, for it is there that you carried three of My children, your body being stretched to do so. The marks you bare and the extra weight you may carry are beautiful to Me. Look at the legs you think are too fat. They are strong and lovely to Me. I gave you those so you could take My love anywhere you'd like to. Look at the hips you think are so wide and the rear you consider to be too big. I love them; to Me, they are absolutely adorable. You see, every last inch of you is lovely to Me. From the moment you arise every morning, I am smiling from ear to ear, for My little girl has awakened to face a new day. Please love yourself, for you are My glory, My masterpiece, My child."

Though my face was wet with tears of the grief I was feeling for all the years I had hated myself, my heart seemed to leap with every word I heard. Hearing the truth right from the lips of the Author of Truth was like liquid life being poured over my soul. I knew that the choice I would now have to make when I looked in the mirror would be a new one. For so many years, it had just been a decision of whether I was going to like myself or not. My decision never involved my Heavenly Father before, but now there was absolutely no denying that He was involved. My decision was now, and would forever be, Am I going to call God a liar? Believing anything other than what He says is true would mean I was choosing to take sides with Satan himself. The decision was easy. I knew I had to accept the Father's perspective of me, and nothing less. If I didn't, I would surely die.

"I will not call you a liar anymore," I told the Father through my tears. "I choose to side with you in all things, including what I think of myself." The words came easily enough, but I still needed to be changed in my heart. By choosing to believe God's Word, I opened the door to freedom from self-loathing. One day at a time from that moment on, my freedom would become more secure as I made the decision to allow God to change me. It wouldn't be easy to block out the shouts of the world—shouts that told me I was less than what I should be. But it would become easier and easier as my view of myself was literally transformed. I began to see myself through Daddy's eyes.

I walked back out onto the balcony, turned my face to the heavens, and smiled. My Heavenly Father had heard my heart's cry and had lovingly arrived to help me. Almost directly before me, waving boldly in the ocean breeze, flew the American flag, a symbol of freedom. I knew that was the Father's last word to me for the night. "You are free," He whispered. The next day, I went shopping with Bill. I bought myself a new bathing suit, and that night, Bill went to the hot tub—with me!

What Daddy Sees

In the beginning, God created the heavens and the earth. He created night and day, the sea and the land, and every living thing on the land. He created fish in the sea, every fruit-yielding tree, every star in the sky, and man. But the very last thing He created, His crowning achievement, so to speak, was Eve, a woman. After He made her, He was finished. She was like the cherry on top of His sundae, the adorning of His creation. And to the Father, she was good.

Daddy loves His girls. He created us to bring forth life. He created us to be the nurturers and nourishers of His family. He made us softer than men, more tender and, most often, more emotionally in tune than men. He made us in His image. Yes, there is a mother's heart in Father God.

> *"O Jerusalem, Jerusalem... how often I wanted to gather your children together, even as a hen gathers her chicks under her wings, but you were not willing." (Matthew 23:37)*
>
> *"As one whom his mother comforts, so I will comfort you; and you shall be comforted in Jerusalem." (Isaiah 66:13)*

The Father created his daughters to be a reflection of a large part of His heart. We are His princesses, and He adores us. When He looks upon us, He does not look at our outward appearances. He looks at our hearts, and there He looks for our beauty, the beauty that He put into us at the beginning of time.

When He looks at us, he sees precious, innocent, little girls. He sees us as we were at age one or two, just beginning to walk on chubby little legs before we became aware that our legs were too big. He looks at our dimples and wrinkles and thinks they are adorable, just as we do when we see a baby girl. From the moment we wake up in the morning to the time we go to sleep at night, our Heavenly Father is absolutely beaming at us. He is proud of his daughters, and we are beautiful beyond words to Him. That's all that matters. It is truly all that matters!

> *"I will praise You; for I am fearfully and wonderfully made; Marvelous are your works, and that my soul knows very well." (Psalm 139:14)*
>
> *"How precious also are Your thoughts to me, O God! How great is the sum of them!" (Psalm 139:17)*

All day long, moment by moment, Father God loves us. All day long, He is whispering in our ears, telling us how beautiful we are to Him. If we would only open our ears, we would hear Him. Or maybe we just need to close our ears to what this world has to say about us. Begin today to close your ears to any message that is contrary to what the Father says about you. The Father does not say you are ugly. The Father does not say you are fat. The Father does not say you are a failure in any way.

The only father who would say cruel things like that is the father of lies. He hates us. He hates God's daughters immensely because he can see how beautiful God made us. Remember, Lucifer was kicked out of heaven because he wanted to be the prettiest.

> *How you have fallen from heaven, O Lucifer, son of the morning! How you are cut down to the ground, you who weakened the nations! For you have said in your heart: I will ascend into heaven, I will exalt my throne above the stars of God; I will also sit on the mount of the congregation on the farthest sides of the north; I will ascend above the heights of the clouds; I will be like the most High. (Isaiah 14:12–14)*

He still wants to be the best, and he'll stop at nothing to blind us from our true beauty that lies within. Stasi Eldredge, in her book, *Captivating*, says "Satan fell *because* of his beauty. Now his heart for revenge is to assault beauty. He destroys it in the natural world wherever he can. Strip mines, oil spills, fires, Chernobyl. He wreaks destruction on the glory of God in the earth like a psychopath committed to destroying works of art. But *most* especially, he hates Eve. Because she is captivating, uniquely glorious, and he cannot be. She is the incarnation of the Beauty of God."

Satan doesn't fight fair. He'll hit you below the belt, wherever it hurts the most. Why would we want to agree with him about anything? Especially when it pertains to our values and identities. Begin today to allow yourself to see the you that God does. Be willing to let Him transform your self-image completely. It may take a little time, but start by being willing to become willing. God will do the rest. He can do it, and He wants to.

Healing Prayer

Dear Heavenly Father,

I cannot even begin to comprehend the deep love You have for me. Thank You for Your kindness. Thank You for Your patience. Thank You for Your grace and neverending mercy. You are my all in all.

Oh, Father, please forgive me for all the years I have called You a liar. I know every time I looked in the mirror and despised what I saw, Your daddy heart must have been crushed. How You must have grieved as You listened to the hateful words that spewed forth from my mouth. Did You feel betrayed when I linked arms with Your enemy? Oh, Father, please forgive me.

Please forgive me for taking all that you created as beautiful and basically spitting upon it. I know that when my own children speak harshly of themselves, it tears my heart apart. What must it have done to You? My heart is filled with godly sorrow over how I have hurt Your heart.

From this day on, I choose to believe You and only You. If You say that I am beautiful, then that is all I need. I will not allow the world's opinions to hold more weight than Yours. How can what this world—so filled with sin and death—says even compare with the words of the Most High God? I have been so deceived.

I choose to allow my heart to be transformed in this area. I choose to close my ears to the lies of my enemy, who is jealous of my beauty—beauty I inherited from Your first daughter, Eve. My beauty has nothing to do with what I weigh. My beauty is based on the One who created me, for You are beautiful. I believe this. I choose to live my life according to this truth from this day on.

Thank You for Your forgiveness, Father. Thank You for Your long-suffering heart, a heart that never fails and never quits seeing the best in Your children. You truly are the best daddy ever, and I am thrilled to be Yours.

You are good! You are good! And Your love endures. Praise You, praise You, praise You.

In my Savior's powerful name,

Amen

CHAPTER EIGHT

SWITCHING ENEMIES

And if a house is divided against itself, that house cannot stand.
-Mark 3:25-

Our week of ministry school was finished, and Bill and I were packed and ready to head home to our precious children. Bill headed out to the hotel lobby to track down a luggage cart, and I made the final sweep through the room to make sure we weren't leaving anything behind. We had packed everything. The only thing I was leaving behind was my self-hatred.

I took one last moment to go out on that special balcony and look out over the magnificent sea. I glanced up at the American flag, waving victoriously in the ocean breeze, and I smiled to myself. Right there, under that flag, I had experienced the beginning of a personal victory like no other.

Though I had come into this week desperately searching for what was keeping me fat, I was leaving with something far greater. God had not revealed to me a deeply hidden root for my consistent failure at diets. He had not supernaturally taken away my appetite so that the pounds would simply begin to melt off of me. He had not convicted me of some hidden sin that was manifesting itself as added weight around my hips. He had simply chosen to reveal what He sees when He looks at me, and for the first time, I had decided to believe Him instead of my lying eyes.

For the first time ever in my life, I had looked at my own reflection and smiled. I don't really know how it happened, but after the Father told me I had been calling Him a liar for so many years, my heart must have been broken enough for him to slip through the cracks and through the tough outer shell. The reflection I saw was no longer of an enemy, but a friend. I saw God's cute, healthy, little girl—not a fat failure of a woman. I saw a glimpse of Daddy's face in mine, and my heart leaped with joy. "I look like my daddy," I thought. "I must be beautiful!"

I walked out of the hotel room thinking to myself, *I'm free. I'm free. I'm really, really free!* I felt like a victorious warrior woman, ready to take on the world. Only days before, I had been suffering under the weight of debilitating self-hatred, but now I was rejoicing and brimming with hope and new life. This was totally new territory for me. For the first time ever, I did not care how much I weighed. I did not spend any time planning what I would eat for the day, and I was not planning on starting a new diet upon arriving home as I always did when returning from vacation. The only plan I had was to live life and live it more than abundantly!

The enemy of my soul wasn't happy about the territory he had lost.

The Oldest Trick in the Book

In the Garden of Eden, Adam and Eve were happy as clams, walking around in all their nakedness before each other and God. They enjoyed true intimacy and an honest relationship, which is what they were created for. But the serpent, which was more cunning than any beast of the field, came upon the scene with a plan to mess that up.

We all know how the story goes. Eve fell for Satan's tactics and was enticed into eating the fruit from the Tree of the Knowledge of Good and Evil. Adam was easily enticed into eating it by Eve. Their eyes were opened for the first time to evil. In essence, they were molested. In their most vulnerable and wounded moment, I believe, the enemy began his job of whispering lies to them. I'm pretty certain I know what the first lie was: "Look at your bodies. You should be ashamed of those."

It is clear that by eating the forbidden fruit, Adam and Eve gained the burden of knowledge that their hearts weren't meant to carry. Their eyes were opened to evil for the first time. For the first time, they understood that they were naked, but for them to feel ashamed of their nakedness, I think the Devil must have spoken a lie to them about the appearance of their bodies.

> *Then the eyes of both of them were opened, and they knew that they were naked; and they sewed fig leaves together and made themselves coverings. And they heard the sound of the Lord God walking in the garden in the cool of the day, and Adam and his wife hid themselves from the presence of the Lord God among the trees of the garden. Then the Lord God called to Adam and said to him, "Where are you?" So he said, "I heard Your voice in the garden, and I was afraid because I was naked; and I hid myself." (Genesis 3:7–10)*

Why did Adam and Eve feel they needed to hide their nakedness from their maker? Didn't they know God had already seen their naked bodies? Of course they did. It wasn't the fact that they were naked that made them hide, but the fact that they saw their nakedness as something to be ashamed of, as something that must be unattractive to God, and that should therefore be hidden.

Of all the lies that Satan could have spoken to Adam and Eve, why did he choose to lie to them about their bodies first? Why not lie to them about their need for a more beautiful home? When God asked Adam where he was, Adam could have replied, "I'm over here, trying to make a roof to put over my family's head. Why didn't you make a better house for us, huh?" Or Adam could have been disappointed in his food options once he had this newfound knowledge. "I'm over here trying to find some prime rib. All these fruits and vegetables are boring. You've been holding out on us," he could have declared.

No, the first thing Satan decided to do was cause God's precious children to feel ashamed of their bodies to hide from God himself. This is the trick Satan has been up to ever since. It's the oldest trick in the book.

An Embarrassing Car

The triune God created His children in his own image. In effect, we are triune, as well. We have a body, soul, and a spirit (1 Thessalonians 5:23). Each part of us has a divine role, a special purpose in God's plan.

According to many theologians, our spirits are the parts of us in which God's Spirit Himself dwells. This is the part that communes with God and can receive His wisdom and truth. It is here that we are made new creatures in Christ once we accept Jesus as our Savior and Lord. This is also the part of us that will live eternally with God after we die.

The soul is the seat of the mind, will, emotions, and personality. This is where we experience God. We may feel goosebumps when we worship, or feel the need to cry because of His amazing goodness to us. Our emotions are also somewhat like the instruments on the dashboard of a car. They alert us to problems that may be occurring in the engine and warn us that we may need some help. There is definitely a purpose for the soul.

Our bodies have important roles, too. Our bodies are meant to be the vehicles that carry our spirits and souls around in this earthly life. Our bodies take us from one place to the next for us to share the love of God with others who may not know Him. Our bodies are meant to carry us around to bring glory to our Heavenly Father by testifying to His mighty works. Our bodies are also meant to be used as God's own flesh on earth. When we get a hug from a brother or sister in Christ, at times it feels like Jesus with flesh on is hugging us.

Though only our spirits are eternal and seemingly most important, they can't go anywhere without vehicles. We can be filled with God's spirit and experience His goodness and love, but if we keep that to ourselves and don't take it anywhere, how is the world going to hear of His goodness? This is exactly what the Devil must have thought to himself right before he told Adam and Eve how ugly their bodies were. "If I can get them ashamed of their bodies," he schemed, "they'll just keep to themselves, and then they won't share the good stuff they know about God. They'll live a life in hiding." This is still the enemy's tactic. He is paralyzing God's children by keeping us disgusted with our bodies. He is tricking us into believing we have ugly "cars" and should just keep them parked in the garage unless we absolutely must go out.

It grieves my heart to think back on all the times I stayed home because I was feeling fat. I can remember times when my husband and children wanted to go swimming and I didn't go because I felt too ugly. I kept my car parked in the garage. I can recall times we were invited to parties and I wouldn't want to go because all my clothes were too tight. I kept the car parked in the garage. I can even remember skipping Bible studies because I was embarrassed about gaining some weight. The car was kept in the garage again. Each time, the Devil got what he wanted. The Holy Spirit within me was trapped in my house. I didn't take it out because I was embarrassed about my car.

There is no doubt that it is important to God that we take care of our bodies. The Bible says that our bodies are the temple of the Holy Spirit: *"Or do you not know that your body is a temple of the Holy Spirit who is in you, whom you have from God, and you are not your own? For you were bought with a price; therefore glorify God in your body and in your spirit, which are God's" (1 Corinthians 6:19–20).*

It is also clear that God does not want food to be a false god to us, because this will lead to gluttony and eventually death: *"You shall have no other gods before Me" (Exodus 20:3).*

Other than those two issues, however, I don't recall ever reading anywhere in the Bible that there is a certain weight we should be or a particular body mass index we should register in at. The only BMI chart I see in God's word is this: Believe Me Immediately! It is not God who set up weight charts and body fat counts. These are standards set in place by someone else. Guess who?

In the Spider's Web

In a way, many of us are like prey caught in a giant spider web. Satan is the big, fat spider sitting atop his web, watching all of his minion spiders spin his victims into nice little meals for him. The big spider doesn't have to do much work anymore, because his system is working like a well-oiled machine. In fact, it's almost on autopilot.

Since the beginning of time, the Devil has been trying to get people's minds distracted by things that don't really matter to keep them from the things that do. He perverts everything that God created to be beautiful and puts counterfeits out there for everything God has meant for our benefit. For example, the Father meant for us to get our need for security met in our relationship with Him. Instead, the Devil tricks us into accepting a counterfeit for that: We believe our security can come from our material possessions or wealth. God meant for us to get our sense of purpose and value from Him and Him alone. The Devil tricks us into believing the counterfeit: that our value comes from what we look like and that our purpose is to look good.

Looking good is not a bad thing. Placing too high a value on it is. Think of this: If someone came into the room holding a dime in his hand and exclaimed, "Look everyone, I found a hundred dollars!" most everyone would tell him that what he really had was merely ten cents. But many of us are like that deceived person. We walk into a room and exclaim, "Look everyone, I've lost 50 pounds!" as if that is worth more than life itself, but the true value of this achievement is far less in the eyes of God.

It's no wonder we place such a high value on being thin. It's plastered everywhere we turn. Satan has a great marketing team. They are on the job! Billboards, magazines, talk shows, and books galore proclaim the value of having a thin body. Commercial after commercial tells us that we should be focusing our attention on getting fat off our bodies. After all, don't we want our spouses to be more attracted to us? Don't we want all the people at the office to be jealous of our amazing bodies? We fall into the trap easily and are spun into the enemy's web.

And while we are obsessing on what our vehicles look like, the cargo stays put in the garage. The Sprit of God dwells in us and is waiting to fill us to overflowing so His love can effect change in the world. God is more concerned with the matters of the heart than He has ever been with the condition of our mortal bodies.

> *"But let it (your beauty) be the hidden person of the heart, with the incorruptible ornament of a gentle and*

quiet spirit, which is very precious to the sight of God." (1 Peter 3:4)

Is it important to be healthy? Yes. But healthy does not mean thin. I am not thin, but I am healthy. I have a healthy blood pressure, good cholesterol levels and blood sugar levels, and I love to get exercise when I have time. I am also 40 to 50 pounds overweight, according to my enemy. I'm not overweight according to my God! I am beautiful to Him, and that is what I choose to focus on from now on! I see the trap, and I don't want to fall into it any more.

I know that as long as my only God is my Heavenly Father, as long as I am not living a lifestyle of gluttony, and as long as I am caring for my body as the temple of the Holy Spirit, I'm doing what God wants me to do with my body. Any other requirements of what I should look like are not coming from Him.

Remember, before the enemy entered the scene in the garden, Adam and Eve were naked and not ashamed. They were not ashamed of their bodies. We need to take back that territory, and once we have it back, we need to be aware of the enemy's schemes and be on the offensive to protect what we've gained.

The Biggest Loser

Satan is a defeated foe. He thought he was winning when he had Jesus crucified, but he was sorely mistaken. Jesus won the battle over sin and death, and by Jesus' death, burial, and resurrection, the way was paved for God's children to be reconciled to Him. Sometime in the future, Satan will be permanently destroyed, but in the meantime, he lurks around, attempting to destroy everyone else.

His only weapon is deception. He cannot change the truth of our position in Christ. We are more than conquerors through Christ. We are justified in Christ. We are members of Christ's body. We are complete in Christ. These statements are the truth of the matter. This is our actual position Biblically. Satan cannot take away from that. But he can try to trick us into believing it's not true.

Satan is able to play tricks with our minds. The Bible makes it clear that even Christians are at risk of being influenced by him. In the book of Acts, Peter confronts Ananias and Sapphira, members of the early church, for their sinful act of deception: *"But Peter said, 'Ananias, why has Satan filled your heart to lie to the Holy Spirit and keep back part of the price of the land for yourself?'" (Acts 5:3).*

This scripture is a warning to us. If we let him, Satan can deceive us. As a matter of fact, that is his primary objective. He is waiting for any and every opportunity to lie to us to keep us ineffective for the kingdom. This is why it is so important for us to make sure our thought lives match up to what the Word says is true.

> *"For the weapons of our warfare are not fleshly, but mighty through God to the pulling down of strongholds, pulling down imaginations and every high thing that exalts itself against the knowledge of God, and bringing into captivity every thought into the obedience of Christ." (2 Corinthians 10:4–5)*

As Christians, we do not need to be afraid of the Devil. We have been given all authority over him through Jesus. The Devil has only the power we give him by believing his lies. That is why it is so important for us to know the truth and live by it. This is why the Word says that knowing the truth sets us free.

> *"And you shall know the truth, and the truth shall make you free." (John 8:32)*
>
> *"I do not pray that You should take them out of the world, but that You should keep them from the evil*

> *one. Sanctify them by Your truth. Your word is truth." (John 17:15, 17)*
>
> *"Finally, brethren, whatever things are true... meditate on these things." (Philippians 4:8)*

One of the enemy's primary goals is to get us to live our lives independent of God. He wants us to try to get our emotional needs met through counterfeits because he knows they lead to death. He truly does want us dead.

If we believe that our worth is directly related to the appearances of our bodies, we are easy prey. This is why people become addicted to plastic surgery or dieting. To feel good about ourselves, we believe we have to fit into the mold made by this world. We easily lose sight of the mold Father God wants us to fill: looking to Christ, who promises to fulfill all of our needs, including our need to feel beautiful.

> *"But my God shall supply all your need according to His riches in glory by Christ Jesus." (Philippians 4:19)*

Standing Strong

If the Devil's only weapon against us is deception, then our biggest weapon against him is truth. As I look back on the healing and freedom that has happened in my life, I see that it has always been a result of God's truth coming in to combat the lies of the enemy. Truth is powerful. We must seek it with all our hearts.

We have to be willing to look into our own hearts and find the areas in which we have been living according to lies. For me, it was a lifetime of believing my life had no value, that I wasn't even worth protecting. I also believed that I needed to perform better for God to truly bless me, and because of that, I was not able to receive the full amount of His love for me.

For you, the lies might be thoughts of worthlessness and shame. Maybe you feel like you've made so many mistakes that God couldn't possibly use you in His kingdom. These are all lies. Any thought that is guilt-inducing, shame-provoking or insecurity-breeding is not from God. His thoughts for us are always full of love, hope, and blessing.

The best time for the enemy to speak his lies to us is when we are vulnerable. We are vulnerable when we are being wounded, when we are over-tired, when we are not in fellowship with other believers, and when we do not know the truth. This is why it is so important for us to get the healing we need for our brokenness and to continue to stay in a place of humility before God and man. We've got to stay dependent on the Father and interdependent with our brothers and sisters in Christ.

As I said before, we do not need to fear the enemy; we just need to understand his tactics and take an active role against them. We need to be ready for him by daily putting on our entire armor and standing strong.

> *Finally, my brethren, be strong in the Lord and in the power of His might. Put on the whole armor of God, that you may be able to stand against the wiles of the devil. For we do not wrestle against flesh and blood, but against principalities, against powers, against the rulers of the darkness of the age, against spiritual hosts of wickedness in the heavenly places. Therefore take up the whole armor of God that you may be able to withstand the evil day, and having done all, to stand. Stand therefore, having girded your waist with truth, having put on the breastplate of righteousness, and having shod your feet with the preparation of the gospel of peace; above all, taking the shield of faith with which you will be able to quench all the fiery darts of the wicked one. And take the helmet of salva-*

tion, and the sword of the Spirit, which is the word of God; praying always with all prayer and supplication in the Spirit, being watchful to this end with all perseverance and supplication for all the saints." (Ephesians 6:10–18)

The belt of truth holds all the other pieces of body armor in place. This is why it is so important to ignore anything that is not from God. Just ignore it. If I hear a thought that is contrary to what I know is truth, I just refuse to dwell on it and then combat it with a thought that is true.

We are to take up the shield of faith. The more we know about our Heavenly Father and the more we experience His love and faithfulness, the more faith we will have. If we want our shields to be substantial, we need to live for opportunities to know Him more and understand His Word.

The helmet of salvation is our assurance that we are blood-bought children of God. If all else fails us in the moment, we can know for sure that we belong to the Father because of what Christ did for us on the cross, and we can rest in the knowledge that we do not belong to this world. We are the Father's, and He will take care of us, not because we deserve it, but because He is that good.

The sword of the spirit is the Word of God. This is our only offensive weapon against the Devil. This does not mean that just waving a Bible around will have power. This means we have to use the Word. We have to speak the Word and believe it. When the Devil tries to tell me I'm fat and ugly, I say out loud, "That's a lie. My Father says I am fearfully and wonderfully made, and He delights in me." In Romans 10:10, Paul says, *"With the heart a man believes resulting in righteousness, but with the mouth he confesses, resulting in salvation."* There is definitely power in our spoken words. The enemy cannot read our minds, so speaking God's truth aloud lets him know that we know the truth.

Finally, we do not overcome the enemy by spending our time focusing on him. We overcome him by spending our time seeking truth. The more truth we internalize and believe, the less we will be tempted to believe lies. Satan would like to keep us bound in our wounding and in our feelings of worthlessness. We have to stand up and say, "No more!" No longer will I live my life as a victim of his lies. No more will I stay paralyzed because I feel inferior according to this world's standards. I am a daughter of the Most High King, and I commit to living my life for Him and Him alone!

Healing Prayer

Dear Heavenly Father,

Once again, I come to You with a heart full of thanksgiving. I thank You for the truth of Your Word that is life to my soul. Thank You that Your Word is steady and unchanging and that it is a rock unto my feet. I love Your Word, and I long to know it more.

Once again, I ask You to forgive me. Forgive me for all the lies of the enemy I have believed in my life. Forgive me for not combating the lies with Your truth and for not using the armor You died to provide for me. I choose to put on that armor now and each day forward.

Humbly, I come to You to admit that it is possible for me to be deceived. I do not have all the answers, and I do not always know what is best for me. I give You permission to convict my heart any time I try to live my life independent of You. When I try to seek comfort from the world's counterfeits of Your blessings, convict me, Lord. When I begin to compare myself to this world's standards, convict me, Lord.

When I find myself striving for the approval of man instead of Your approval, convict me, Lord. When I start to feel like no good thing will ever come to me and that I need to fight for all I can get, convict me, Lord. Any time I fall short of the lines You have drawn for me, I give You permission to convict me. I long to live within the boundaries You have set, for I know that they are safety and life.

Today I confess aloud that Satan will have no hold on me. I renounce any past lies I have believed, and I confess that I will be a warrior of truth from this day forward. I proclaim to the wind that my God is not this world and that no weapon formed against me shall prosper. If God be for me, who can be against me? No one! I can do all things through Christ. I can know the truth and be set free. I am more than a conqueror. Anything else is a lie. I choose not to believe lies any more.

Fill me more this day with your unconditional love, Father. I know that it is Your perfect love that will cast out any fear in me, and I know that it is Your goodness that will draw me to further repentance. I open my heart to receive all that You have to give to me, and I receive it with gladness.

I love You and praise You with all I have to give. Take my will and conform it to Yours, dear Lord. I surrender all.

In Jesus' precious name,

Amen

CHAPTER NINE

A FAILURE NO MORE

I may never march down your runways,
Wear your bikinis,
Be on your magazines;
I may never fit your ideal for me,
But I'm in the Lord's Army,
Yes, sir!

God wants His children to be free. Ever since the time of the great Exodus when Moses led the children of Israel out of Egyptian bondage, the Father has been at work seeking to free His people from the influence and oppression of false gods. He is still longing to do this today. I believe if we would stop to listen, we would hear Him saying still, "Let my people go!"

The god of this world, Satan, wants us to bow down to the idol of outward beauty and the image of sensuality that he presents. He longs to keep us in slavery to his false idols, desperately serving the systems of this world. But again, the Father says, "Let my people go!"

The Father is waiting for His children to run into the welcome of His outstretched arms. He is longing to pour over us His endless love and words of affirmation. He is longing for us to see ourselves as He does, beautiful and perfect in Christ. I'm so thankful the blinders have been taken off of my eyes. I am so thankful that my life has been saved, and for the first time ever, I am thankful to be me!

When I look into the mirror, I smile. Not because I've finally lost weight. I haven't lost a pound. I smile because I see myself as extremely valuable to my Heavenly Father. I smile because I don't hate myself any more. I smile because I am free.

If my clothes feel a little tight some days, I just say, "Oh well!" It has nothing to do with my worth as a person and definitely nothing to do with what God can do through me today if I let Him. Instead of waiting until I lose weight to treat myself to a new pair of pants, I buy them for myself today. Instead of feeling so bad about myself that I stay home, I put on another pair of pants that are more comfortable, and I embrace the world. I am not going to miss out on anything else.

When I'm in the checkout lane at the grocery store and I'm surrounded by glamour magazines covered with images of what the world thinks is beautiful, I just smile and thank God that I don't fall for those lies anymore. I would rather be free from the enemy's big web than live my life striving to look like the airbrushed images before me. I grieve because I see the world walking around thinking a dime is worth one hundred dollars. Outward beauty is so fleeting, so vain. What I finally have is eternal. The freedom I have has far greater value than physical beauty ever could.

What makes me sad is looking back on all the years I kept myself from truly engaging in life, all the years I felt inferior and self-conscious because my body didn't look the way I thought it should. What makes me sad is seeing myself as a little girl being lied to and bullied by the enemy of my soul. But that is over. I refuse to be bullied by a big liar anymore. I am reclaiming what was mine all along. I am reclaiming my inheritance in Christ and choosing to embrace my future with my head held high.

Back in the Game

Before my journey to freedom began, 80% of my thought life was consumed with negative thoughts about myself. Even if I was doing something that seemed fun, my self-hatred was always lurking behind the scenes. Now, I don't spend time thinking bad things about myself. I don't waste my time thinking thoughts that would come in agreement with the enemy of my soul. Remember, I'm not going to call God a liar any more.

Eighty percent of my thought life is freed up for other things. It's amazing. I feel more love for others than I ever felt before. I am more sincerely interested in the blessings of others than I ever was before. I long to keep short accounts with God and people, asking for forgiveness when I have sinned and walking in right relationship when it is up to me.

I don't waste time in bitterness or resentment. If I sense any of that creeping in, I just confess it to the Father and move on. I don't waste time thinking about how many calories I've consumed and pouting about what I can't eat. I don't resent others who can eat things I've denied myself. I don't judge others according to what they weigh, either. Praise God for that! When I look at another woman, I choose to see a daughter of God, not a thin or fat person. I'm not compelled to compare myself to everyone any more. I'm just happy to be me.

I don't spend time worrying about what other people think of my size any more, either. It doesn't really matter if they think I'm overweight. The only opinion that truly matters to me now is God's. If I sense that He is pleased with what He sees, that's all that matters. Because I don't need the approval of man, I'm not devastated when I don't get it.

It is amazing to me that a series of simple revelations could bring about such transformation in my life. Starting with a new understanding of the Father's heart for me and continuing with more revelations of His truth, this road is one I never want to depart from.

Thankful for my Big Butt

I know without a shadow of a doubt that if I had been given a skinny body from birth, I would not be where I am today. If God had chosen to give me a naturally thin frame, I would have flaunted my stuff daily. I know I would have.

If I had lived my life with a sexy body according to what the world says, I would have received my sense of value and worth from my looks. I would have enjoyed the attention a perfect body would have brought to me, and I would have lived my life in many ways independent of God. I would not have really needed Him. I just know myself.

I can look back on all the years of pain and agony, all the tears I cried begging God to change my body, all the journal entries crying out for answers to my weight problems, and I now can say, "Thank you, God." I can't imagine a life without the freedom I now have. Being thin could never compare to the victory I can claim.

I might have lost weight, but what is being thin without an understanding of the Father's true love for me? I might have worn a smaller size, but how would that heal my wounded heart? No, I thank God for my big rear. My hatred of my own flesh kept me on my face before Him, crying for mercy. My hatred of my own flesh kept me reaching out to Jesus for salvation. Even though I was looking for God to change my body, at least I was looking for God. If I had been thin, I'm not sure that I would have been looking to Him much.

My big rear led me to want to die. My desire to die led my husband to bring me to Chicago. That Chicago trip opened my eyes to the Father's love for me in a new way. His love led me to understand my orphan-heart issues. His love for me led me to greater healing than I've ever experienced in deeply wounded parts of my heart. My healing led me to trust Him enough to ask Him to show me all the ugly roots within me. My willingness to see the truth allowed Him to show me I had been calling Him a liar all of my life. My repentance led the way for me to accept His truth about who I am and what my true value is.

My big butt thus led me to a life that is more than abundant. I am forever thankful for this rear of mine. If someone could wave a magic wand today and make this offer: "You can be fifty pounds thinner in an instant, but you will lose the knowledge of the Father's heart toward you," I know I would turn it down. Nothing, absolutely nothing, can compare to the victory I now have.

I love my big butt! I no longer feel like a failure, because I know that weight loss was never God's plan for me. It was freedom that He had in mind all along. He knew that for me, weight loss would have been a temporary peace. He wanted me to have the peace that passes all understanding. It is truly hard for me to understand why I feel such peace now. All I know is that I praise God for making me who I am, and I intend to keep this vehicle out of the garage from now on!

Where Are You?

Maybe you are reading this and thinking my story seems too good to be true. Well, the fact that it happened for me is proof that it's not. There is no reason for me to love myself today except that we have a Daddy who is amazing. He absolutely adores His daughters, and He lives to bring life to us.

Right now, no matter what you weigh or what you look like, the Father is proud of who you are. He is smiling upon you and loving every inch of you. He longs for you to be free and healthy. He longs to pour upon you His amazing, unconditional love. If you will begin to receive it, it will transform your life. Day by day, moment by moment, His perfect love will set you free.

Each of our journeys will be different. Some of us have been wounded for many years. The healing process may require more time and the help of trained ministry workers or professionals. But it is the Father's will for His children to be free. It is for freedom that Christ died—not just freedom from hellfire and brimstone, but freedom from the power and influence of the god of this world and his minions. The Father longs for you to receive His love, to begin to love yourself, and then to be able to love all the others he puts into your life. We can never truly love our families, friends, or neighbors if we don't love ourselves. We can never love ourselves without God's truth. The devil does not want us to love ourselves. It is his plan to keep us feeling ugly and unlovable. He will stop at nothing to keep us paralyzed in self-loathing.

We all have the freedom of choice. We can choose this day whom we will serve. Will we continue to bow down to the idols of this world, giving value to what the Devil says deserves value, or will we choose to base our value system on what the Creator of Heaven and Earth deems valuable? One is a liar; the other is the Author of Life. It seems like a pretty simple decision.

Let us rise up and believe our Heavenly Father. We, His beautiful daughters, have an irreplaceable role in His kingdom. Let us walk boldly, unashamed of who we are, into the plans He has for us—plans not for calamity, but for a future and a hope!

A Prayer of Thanksgiving

Dearest Father God,

I am thankful today, not only for who You are, but for who You have made me to be. Thank You for planning my life, and for creating me according to Your perfect will.

I thank You for every blessing in my life but also for every wound. My wounds have made me able to understand another's pain. I thank You for every victory but also every failure, for my failures caused me to cry out to You for help. I thank You for every friend but also for every enemy, for it is my enemies who have taught me the value of forgiveness. I thank You for the times that things seem easy but also for the difficult times, for it is those times that have brought me into a deeper relationship with You. I thank You for Your sovereignty, Lord. You are so worthy of my praise.

I thank You for my new ability to love myself. It is a jewel of great price. I thank You that when I look in the mirror, I see Your reflection more and more each day, and not that of an enemy. I thank You that I can even see my flaws as cute distinctions to You—the very things that make me uniquely me. I'm thankful that the parts of my body that used to disgust me are no longer a source of pain to me. Your love covers my imperfections, and in that I find my refuge.

I thank You that I can crawl up into Your loving arms any time I feel the enemy seeking to trap me again. I thank You that all I need do is look up into Your loving gaze, and it is there that truth will be restored to me—instantly. I thank You that You are my protector, that I can hide beneath the shelter of Your wings. Thank You for being my hiding place when things get tough. Thank You that I can always run boldly to Your throne of grace. You are amazing.

Father, I thank You from the bottom of my heart for not answering my prayers in the ways I always wished You would. Thank You for knowing full well exactly what I truly needed. I joyfully accept Your answer to my prayers. I asked for bread; You gave me a feast. You are such an amazing daddy.

I love You and long to receive more of who You are each day. I want to know You more. I want to know You more.

In Jesus' victorious name,

Amen

Acknowledgments

I might truly be dead right now if it weren't for the love and blessing of the following people, and without them I would never have written this book.

My precious husband, Bill: Thank you for lowering me through the roof when I was on my deathbed. If not for your desperate love for me, I'm not sure where I would be. You are my best friend.

Our dear friends James and Dawn Taylor: It's as if you had the exact cure for my fatal disease. I know our Father sent you into my life. Thank you for your unfailing encouragement and the unspeakable joy of being kindred spirits.

To the late Jack Frost, his wife Trisha, and the ministry team at Shiloh Place: How can I thank you enough? Jack was the most transparent man I have ever met, and his transparency and willingness to be real helped me to drop my walls and receive what the Father was trying to give me all along.

To my pastor, Steve Berger, and his wife, my friend, Sarah: Thank you for loving me through so many stages of my spiritual and emotional growth. Thank you for your words of encouragement and for believing the best about me when I wasn't always my best. Thank you for being an example of living a life hard after God no matter what. Your example has instilled in me a desire to be nothing but a warrior for truth.

My dear childhood friends, Christina Broadwin, Suzy Foley, Michelle Rajcic, and Tracy Stanley, and my baby sister and brother, Jenny Fann and Joey Gootee: How can I thank you enough for putting up with me and loving me when I know I wasn't very loveable? Thank you for listening to all my diet plans and being there for me when they failed. I love you.

Thank you to my sweet "Cannon Family," especially my precious mother and father-in-law, Martha and Terry Cannon. Your unconditional love and acceptance of me into your family continues to be a blessing. I also want to say a special thank you to my sister-in-law, Sunny Rosanbalm, for her love and perfect artwork on the cover of this book.

And to my amazing church family at Grace Chapel: I love you and thank you for loving me. Thank you to Pastors Jonathan Allen, Rick Cua, Jake Spencer, Jim Sterling, and Jay Tremblay for your encouragement and wise counsel.

Thank you to my "bosom friends" who have loved me without end for years: Allison Allen, Colleen Daly, Jodie Grenead, Barb Mahy, Stephanie Reifsnyder, and Tracy Stanley. You are the best friends anyone could ask for, and I can't thank God enough for you.

To Phil Stoner: thank you so very much for being the first to read the manuscript of this book and for your continual encouragement and advice. I also thank God for the friendship and encouragement of the following people regarding this book and my passions: Lisa Patton Brown, Pat Clonts, Meg Cox, Diana Cua, Deanna Dolan, Lark Foster, Susanne Haven, Lona Heinz, Anne Marie Helmsworth, Wynonna Judd, Amy Lowry, Debby Pasch, Camille Piland, Diane Spencer, Byron Spradlin, Tracy Sterling, Linda Yoder, and Wes Yoder.

Mom and Dad: You are such a huge blessing to me. Mom, thank you for being a prayer warrior and an example of what it looks like to love God with your whole heart. Dad, thank you for being an example of unconditional love and encouragement. Your example made it so much easier for me to accept the love of my Heavenly Father. Thank you both for knowing I would someday write a book and for your input into this one.

My precious children: Carli, you are my beauty from ashes, and I adore you. Thank you for being a merciful daughter as I have gone through some of my most painful days. You are such a good girl. Ben and Sam, thank you for adoring me always, and thank you for being so cuddly. You are mighty men of God!

To my sweet grandma, Johnnie B. Parker, in heaven with our Daddy: thank you for loving me and for passing down the genes that gave me my big butt blessing! I can't wait to kiss your face again someday.

And last but always first, Father God: Thank you for knowing me so well and giving me everything I need. Thank you for saving my life, not only for heaven, but for my time here on earth. You are my heart's desire and my first love.

LaVergne, TN USA
12 April 2010
179041LV00001B/5/P